Welcome

Britain's V Bombers are fondly remembered. And with good reason.

Forming Britain's nuclear shield during the 1950s and '60s, it is hard to overestimate the value of service the V-Force provided for the UK.

As Britain emerged from the agony of World War Two and began to look to the new opportunities ahead, Winston's Churchill's famous 'Iron Curtain' descended, and the country was plunged into a new type of arms race to protect its freedoms. Aviation was arguably the biggest beneficiary of developing technology during the 1950s and '60s; it was certainly an era when everything seemed to be 'bigger, faster and higher' than the world had seen before, and the V-Bombers certainly fitted into that category. Rapidly improving jet engine performance meant piston-powered bombers were rendered obsolete as the new jet generation took over. Given the emphasis on the 'space race' of the day, it is no surprise that V-Bombers had a certain 'science fiction' look about them and their sheer size, shape and noise levels turned heads everywhere

they went. The Handley Page Victor was certainly a unique shape in the sky.

Only a handful of British aircraft types can rival the level of public admiration held by Britain's V-Bombers and this was surely proven by the recent, ambitious, spectacular, but relatively shorted-lived return from retirement afforded to Vulcan XH558. It drew tens of thousands of people out to see its displays up and down the country and attracted donations like no restoration before it.

In this tribute to the men and machines of V-Force, I have deliberately steered away from covering the development aircraft, the likes of the Avro 707 and H.P.88 in order to devote more space to 'the real thing' and I hope you will enjoy the end result.

Tom Allett
Editor

ABOVE: **The classic, clean lines of the first V-Bomber, the Vickers Valiant B.1, are evident it this 1950s photograph.** (KEY Archive)

Editor: Tom Allett
Senior editor, specials: Roger Mortimer
Email: roger.mortimer@keypublishing.com
Design: Dan Jarman
Cover design: Steve Donovan

Advertising Sales Manager: Brodie Baxter
Email: brodie.baxter@keypublishing.com
Tel: 01780 755131

Advertising Production: Rebecca Antoniades
Email: rebecca.antoniades@keypublishing.com

SUBSCRIPTION/MAIL ORDER
Key Publishing Ltd, PO Box 300,
Stamford, Lincs, PE9 1NA
Tel: 01780 480404 Fax: 01780 757812
Subscriptions email: subs@keypublishing.com
Mail Order email: orders@keypublishing.com
Website: www.keypublishing.com/shop

DISTRIBUTION
Seymour Distribution Ltd, 2 Poultry Avenue,
London, EC1A 9PU
Enquiries Line: 02074 294000.

PRINTING
Precision Colour Printing Ltd, Haldane,
Halesfield 1, Telford, Shropshire. TF7 4QQ

PUBLISHING
Group CEO: Adrian Cox
Publisher: Mark Elliott
Head of Publishing: Finbarr O'Reilly
Chief Publishing Officer: Jonathan Jackson
Key Publishing Ltd, PO Box 100, Stamford,
Lincs, PE9 1XP Tel: 01780 755131
Website: www.keypublishing.com

COVER IMAGE:
RAF Avro Vulcan B2 XH558, part of the RAF Vulcan Display Flight taken in 1992.
(KEY Archive)

Contents

Weapons of Mass Destruction

Tom Allett looks at the bombs and bombers from the dawn of the nuclear arms race.

The World War-winning nuclear strikes upon Hiroshima and Nagasaki in August 1945 focused the superpowers' minds on a new type of arms race.

Even before the devastation was fully understood by anyone outside of those cities, the speed at which the Japanese government then surrendered to the Allies made it obvious that a new magnitude of destruction was now possible.

Militarily speaking, in a matter of days the world was effectively divided into two camps, the United States and its allies who had the bomb, against potential adversaries who did not.

Nevertheless, despite the closeness of the US-UK relationship forged during World War Two, Britain was soon facing the prospect of having to develop its own nuclear weapons as national security concerns led the US into a new period of isolationism.

Despite America's post-war isolationist stance regarding the development of nuclear weapons, Britain's participation in the US' wartime nuclear bomb programme, the *Manhattan Project* set it on course to become the world's third nuclear power. However, Britain needed to develop a delivery system too as it had no recognised nuclear capable bomber. The RAF's legendary Avro Lancaster had been briefly considered for delivering what became the Hiroshima bomb, code named *Fat Man*, but even long before the weapon was ready, the US authorities had insisted that its delivery must be made by an American aircraft. With hindsight, given the bomb's dimensions it would not have fitted into the Lancaster's bomb bay without major modifications. Even then, its bulbous shape would have protruded significantly from under the fuselage and appreciably degraded the Lancaster's range and altitude performance. The long flight – approximately six hours – was likely beyond >>

BELOW: **The world's first nuclear explosion, that of the so-called Trinity bomb, took place at 0529 on July 16, 1945. The use of two similar strength devices against Hiroshima and Nagasaki the following month brought World War Two to an abrupt halt.** (US Department of Energy via Wikimedia)

an aerodynamically impaired Lancaster, and a required bomb release height of 32,000ft made the odds of success even more unlikely. While the then new Avro Lincoln offered a slight performance improvement, it was not enough to make the Lancaster's successor a candidate for nuclear duties. That task would fall to the emerging jets and the changing political landscape of the emerging Cold War meant the targets would now be in the Soviet Union.

CHICKEN AND EGG SITUATION

In the immediate post-war period, even if Britain had had nuclear bombs, it had no means of delivering them and vast sums of money would be required to develop both at a time when the country was still subject to the rationing of goods, similar to what the general public had endured from 1939-45. Despite the country's depressed financial state, the need to keep its theoretical superpower status outweighed the country's austere circumstances. Which should be prioritised, the bomb or the delivery method?

In August 1946, the British Cabinet had signalled the necessity – via Air Staff Operational Requirement OR.1001 – for the creation of a bomb 'employing the principal of nuclear fission'. Given the secrecy surrounding atomic weapons, the requirement was understandably vague about such things as explosive power, dimensions, and weight. More time and research were needed to establish what was possible and the government did not give formal approval for developing a fission bomb until 1947. After extensive studies, the Requirement was reissued in 1948 and gave direction about the 'vital statistics'. It called for a bomb that did not exceed 290in in length, a diameter of 60in, weight no greater than 10,000lb and was capable of being released from between 20,000-50,000ft at speeds ranging from 150-500kts. The resulting weapon would almost certainly be too large and heavy for even the largest RAF aircraft in service and missile technology could not yet deliver such a warhead. Britain's Air Ministry agreed that new aircraft would be required and OR.230 was issued requiring a 'landplane capable of carrying one 10,000lb bomb to a target 2,000nm from a base situated anywhere in the world'.

Because it would surely have to confront enemy radar defences, it would need to be capable of flying at extremely high altitude – between 35,000 and 50,000ft – and high speed, some 500kts. Although it would be expected to carry electronic countermeasures for its own protection, no self-defence gun turrets would be provided as they would

add greatly to the weight of the aircraft and therefore inhibit its speed and altitude performance. Even without defensive armament, the new aircraft was expected to be heavy, with an all-up weight of 200,000lbs. It was unlikely the new machine would be capable of operating from existing RAF airfields, most of which had wartime runways of 6,000ft or shorter.

Even if a suitable aircraft could somehow have been developed, its cost would potentially be so high that the government would probably only be able to supply the RAF with a handful of operational airframes, making the envisaged operational task impractical. Given these hurdles, the Air Ministry eventually decided that it would settle for an aircraft that could deliver a single nuclear device to Moscow. Anything beyond that capability would be regarded as a bonus. This led to another Operational Requirement OR.229 being issued, together with Specification B.35/46. This time any new aircraft would still be required to carry the original 10,000lb weapon, and meet the previously declared altitude, but the required range was reduced to a comparatively modest 1,500nm. Nevertheless, this still represented a huge leap in aircraft capability, and some thought it would be necessary to build half-scale models first. One thing that seemed clear was that whichever company produced the best design would receive a highly lucrative contract so, after receiving invites to tender, Britain's aircraft manufacturers drew up their plans.

The Air Ministry invited Handley Page, Vickers Armstrongs, Avro, Bristol, Shorts of Belfast and, slightly later, English Electric to provide design submissions. A design tender conference was subsequently arranged, and Avro's submission was identified as the strongest contender, although the meeting also agreed that either the Handley Page or Armstrong Whitworth designs should also be taken-up (together with flying models) but only if high-speed wind tunnel research by the Royal Aircraft Establishment (RAE) found them to be promising.

The RAE considered Handley Page's crescent-wing design to be even more revolutionary than Avro's delta but, later, it was Avro and Handley Page's designs that received the financial support necessary to move ahead. All the other proposals were all rejected with the Air Ministry considering those from Vickers Armstrongs and English Electric to be 'unimaginative' but given that the latter was already heavily committed to developing the Canberra medium-range jet bomber, perhaps it was

ABOVE: **Although the Avro Lincoln was an improvement upon its wartime Lancaster predecessor, its performance still fell far short of what was required to survive in the jet era.** (KEY Archive)

LEFT: **Boeing B-29 *Enola Gay* dropped the Hiroshima bomb on August 5, 1945 and introduced a new level of arms race.** (USAF)

impractical for that company to be running two such major programmes simultaneously.

Despite all the visionary work undertaken, the reality was that few at the Air Ministry had great confidence in these innovative designs actually achieving the required performance and so a further design specification (B.14/46) was issued. This was deemed to be an 'insurance' design that would provide an admittedly inferior aircraft than desired, should the original choices fail to meet the required standards. At the very least, it should ensure that the RAF had a jet bomber.

The 'insurance' design would reflect tried and trusted technology such as straight - instead of swept – wings and a conventional tail unit. The Belfast-based Short Brothers and Harland company won the contract to provide it with a 'safe' design that was not hugely different from its earlier submission. Named the Short Sperrin (after the mountains of the same name), two prototypes were built and flown, meaning that three different nuclear jet bomber types were simultaneously under development. Vickers-Armstrongs, having also seen the potential for failure amongst the Avro and Handley Page designs, put forward its own proposal for an 'insurance' aircraft that could meet the weapon

delivery criteria using a more conventional design. When accepted, there were then – incredibly – four jet nuclear bombers being developed at the same time. However, the Sperrin's performance fell far short of the RAF's requirements and its development as a bomber was halted. Instead, they were used to gather research data of several types of jet engines. Both were retired in the late 1950s and eventually scrapped.

As the selected designs progressed, a small-scale development aircraft, the HP.88, was built to explore the company's striking design. Sadly, it crashed with fatal results, but it was thought that enough data had been acquired to know that what would become the H.P. Victor was a viable machine. Avro also built several small development aircraft – the Avro 707 series – which successfully provided vital knowledge about delta wing performance characteristics and paved the way for the Vulcan prototypes that followed. Vickers, having also gained funding for its 'insurance' jet, pushed ahead with its more conventional model, which would later be named Valiant. While these embryonic airframes were under development, the British government was simultaneously building its first atomic bombs. But where could they be assessed? »

SUITABLE SITES

Lacking large open and sparsely populated areas at home, Britain sought permission from overseas governments to conduct its first nuclear bomb tests. In 1952 the Australian government gave its consent for a detonation at the Montebello Islands off the northwest coast of Australia. There, on October 3, in *Operation Hurricane*, Britain detonated its first atomic bomb – a plutonium implosion device – in the Bay's shallow waters. The trial was deemed both a technological and scientific success, but to be a true-nuclear power, Britain still needed a tried and tested delivery method. A year later, in October 1953, the first nuclear test on the Australian mainland took place at Emu field in the Great Victoria Desert in southern Australia. Part of *Operation Totem*, it was the first of two A-bombs exploded at ground level along with four conventional explosions that assessed the efficiency of the nuclear bombs' initiators, which 'kick-started' the chain reaction process that would lead to the ultimate detonation. After the two detonations, Avro Lincoln bombers were used to perform several sweeps through the towering debris clouds to collect air samples.

Next in the bomb-development series was *Operation Mosaic* which comprised two nuclear tests. The scientists considered the previous Emu Field location unsuitable for further detonations and sought a more permanent spot for their experiments. A new site at Maralinga, also in southern Australia, was selected but the amount of preparation work required meant that it would not be ready in time. As a compromise the test teams returned to the Montebello Islands. Mosaic's primary purpose was to determine how to increase the yield of the British devices. Its two detonations, on May 16 and June 19, 1956, both involved boosted fission weapons. Technically, these were not hydrogen bombs – the British government had agreed those would not be tested in Australia – but they did form part of Britain's evolving hydrogen bomb programme. There remains an unanswered question about the second *Mosaic* bomb. The agreement between the respective governments allowed for explosive yields up to the equivalent of 50 kilotonnes of TNT. Originally, the second detonation was recorded at approximately 60 kilotonnes, but later studies estimated the figure was close to 100 kilotonnes – uncharted territory for a British weapon of the day. However, a definitive measurement has never been established.

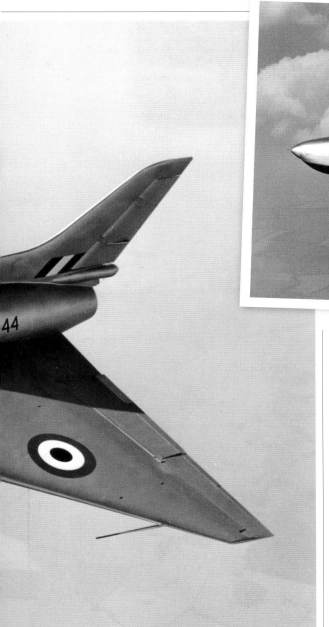

BUFFALO

Britain's bomb programme had made enough progress to be fairly sure that its first air-drop was almost within reach. With the preparation work at the Maralinga site now complete, the programme could move back to the desert. The site lay within the giant Woomera Prohibited Area which also had a role as a missile testing zone – some 500 miles north of Adelaide.

Operation Buffalo comprised four major tests of Britain's *Blue Danube* bomb plus more than 500 smaller experiments focused upon efficiency.

The first two major explosions – at the sites named One Tree and Breakaway – were similar to the Hiroshima bomb in terms of explosive power (but not design) and detonated while attached to towers. The blast at the third location, named Marcoo, was much smaller by comparison but took place at ground level. However, progression to the final major explosion required a huge leap forward as it was the first air-drop. That detonation of a *Blue Danube* bomb within the Maralinga range on October 11, 1956, delivered an explosive yield of about three kilotonnes and proved the RAF was capable of a nuclear airdrop at the first time of asking. (See page 14 for more details)

ABOVE: **Worried that the ambitious modern designs from Avro and Handley Page might not succeed, the Air Ministry invested in an 'insurance policy' – the Short Sperrin, an aircraft with a more conventional design – which would ensure that the RAF had a jet bomber of some sort. Although two Sperrins were built, their performance fell below requirements, and they were relegated to engine test duties before being scrapped.**
(KEY Archive)

LEFT: *Yellow Sun* was the first British operational high-yield strategic nuclear weapon. The name refers only to the outer casing; the warhead (or physics package) was known as *Green Grass* in *Yellow Sun* Mk.1 and *Red Snow* in *Yellow Sun* Mk.2.
(Tom Oates)

Vickers' Fearless Cold War Bomber

The leader of the V-Bomber pack - the Vickers Valiant.
By **William Noble**

During the latter stages of World War Two the incredible success of a small, high-speed, high-altitude bomber in the shape of the de Havilland Mosquito was not lost on senior Air Staff. However, the immediate plan for the future of RAF Bomber Command still lay in the fundamentals of heavily defended bombers, complete with unpressurised accommodation for the crew, the Avro Lincoln and Vickers Windsor being penned in for the post-war role. Only the former would enter service and, in the meantime, a new philosophy, influenced by advances in the turbojet engine and availability of a nuclear weapon, completely changed Air Staff thinking, rendering the Lincoln little more than a stop-gap solution.

The idea that a lone aircraft could deliver a single weapon which could cause more devastation than a wartime thousand-bomber raid, was very appealing to a post-war government, whose main priority was restoration of the economy. The turbojet had the ability to deliver a huge increase in power over traditional piston engines, potentially enabling very high altitudes with crews contained within pressurised cabins, it was a subject that Vickers was well ahead of the game with, thanks to its trials work with the Vickers Wellington V and VI and their pressurised fuselages. In theory there would be no need for defensive armament and newly developed electronic equipment would make high speed, high ceiling bombing feasible.

The Air Staff now had a concept to work with, which would take Bomber Command forward into the jet age with a much lower number of aircraft capable of carrying the full range of ordnance available, plus the all-important nation's nuclear deterrent. Both political and military philosophy of the day liked the idea of a much smaller, yet more powerful Bomber Command. However, the cost of producing such technologically advanced aircraft was high and the Treasury would restrict production numbers.

The idea of this new Bomber Command was also supported by the public, which fully backed a new rearmament drive making the country a world player when it came to nuclear weapons. Although Britain did not have its own nuclear weapon during the immediate post-war period, there was an assumption that they would initially be provided by the USA in recognition of the amount of work conducted by British scientists during the World War Two. In the meantime, Britain would continue to develop its own nuclear weapons.

THE SPECIFICATIONS

By late 1945 a pair of bomber aircraft Operational Requirements (OR) were issued; OR.229 (Medium Range) and OR.230 (Long Range). Both called for an aircraft capable of slipping past enemy defences at high altitude, escaping interception with high speed and being able to drop a nuclear weapon. Both requirements were thrown open to leaders of the aviation industry, with the main focus being on OR.229, Armstrong Whitworth, Avro, Bristol de Havilland, English Electric, Handley Page, Short and Vickers, all expressing an interest. The requirements were shaped into Specification B.35/46 on January 24, 1947. This specifically called for an aircraft capable of carrying a single 10,000lb 'special weapon' or the equivalent weight in conventional weapons over 3,600 miles. Six tenders were presented, four of which were good enough to warrant the order of prototype machines. While the designs produced by Avro and Handley Page were deemed as radical, those accepted by Vickers and Shorts were seen as less so. Of the latter the design presented by Shorts and later named ▶▶

ABOVE: **WB210 is seen Landing at the 1951 SBAC show at Farnborough. The aircraft was used for tests until January 1952, when it was lost after an in-flight fire.**

MAIN PICTURE: **The gleaming prototype Valiant, WB210, was ordered in 1949 and first flew from the grass airfield at Wisley in 1951.** (KEY Archive)

the Sperrin, was by far the inferior design, but could be produced the quickest and as such, served as an insurance policy should one of the other three designs fail.

Vickers' initial design for a high-performance bomber was not actually accepted purely because it could not meet the requirement for range, however, it could accomplish all the other criteria and, being less technically advanced than the Avro and Handley Page designs and be delivered much more quickly to Bomber Command. On that point alone the Vickers submission was very appealing, so a new specification, B.9/48 was drawn up around the aircraft, which would become the Type 660 in the company design list. On February 2, 1949, two prototypes were ordered, the Type 660 to be powered by four Rolls-Royce Avon RA3 turbojets and the second aircraft, the Type 667, would be fitted with a quartet of Armstrong Siddeley Sapphire turbojets.

Design work began in 1949 and by 1950, work had progressed where components were being built into main assemblies at the company's Foxwarren experimental shop – a dispersal factory from the main Weybridge site in Surrey. All under the direction of prototype manager, A W E 'Charlie' Houghton, progress was swift and final assembly of the first prototype started at Wisley in early 1951.

NUTS AND BOLTS!

The Vickers Type 660 was far from being an inferior design compared to the more dramatic looking Vulcan and Victor. The austere years following the end of World War Two were not an easy period to produce such an advanced aircraft, but Vickers pulled it off and the Valiant was the prettiest of the three V-bombers. The primary structure of the aircraft was a substantial 'backbone' which extended the full length of the fuselage. To this, were attached light-alloy tensile formers, spaced off with high-tensile stringers all of which was covered by a very neat flush-rivetted stressed skin. The shoulder-wing design lent itself to a cavernous bomb bay (the only V-bomber capable of carrying the Blue Steel missile fully internally) and the same 'backbone' was used to carry the weapon load. The 'backbone' branched at right angles, incorporating ring frames (aka branch spars) that wrapped around the turbojets, which, in typical British style, were buried tidily within the inner wing. The engine intakes of the first prototype were straight-slot type and the jet pipes were shorter for the Avon RA.3 engines; all other aircraft had larger intakes and marginally longer jet pipes. From the branch spars, the outer wing spars were attached, the wing itself having a compound sweepback of the leading edge which provided a large root chord that made sufficient room for the buried Avon engines.

The standard crew of five (although the Valiant could carry seven) was accommodated in a large, pressurised cabin which was manufactured by Saunders-Roe. As with all V-bombers, only the pilot and co-pilot were equipped with Martin Baker 3a (later upgraded) ejector seats, the remainder of the crew would have to make their escape through the main crew door, which at least had a wind shield to deflect the slipstream and make an emergency departure more survivable.

The large swept fin was complemented by a swept tailplane which was mounted halfway up the former, well clear of the engine efflux. Regarding the undercarriage, the nosewheel was fairly conventional while the main units where more complex. Each unit consisted of dual legs and wheels arranged in tandem and retracted sideways and outwards. Like most of the aircraft systems, the undercarriage retracted electrically via an actuator and worm gearing. The only systems in the aircraft that were hydraulic were the brakes and nosewheel steering gear, although the pumps for these were still driven by electric motors.

BELOW: **The second prototype Vickers Valiant, WB215, in an all-silver finish. The aircraft was at the forefront of flight testing following the loss of WB210.**

ABOVE: **Whilst the Valiant was originally envisaged a high-altitude bomber, its re-role to a low-attack portfolio would prove to be its undoing when metal fatigue weakened the airframes.** (KEY Archive)

THE PROTOTYPES

Serialled WB210, the prototype Vickers Type 660 made its maiden flight, with 'Mutt' Summers at the controls and Gabe Robb 'Jock' Bryce in the right-hand seat, from the grass runway at Wisley on May 18, 1951. It was a successful, albeit short maiden flight which was followed by just three more before flight testing was transferred to Hurn so a concrete runway could be built at Wisley. In June 1951, the aircraft was officially named the Valiant, a re-use of the name allocated to the 1931 Type 131 biplane.

Flight testing continued from Hurn, but WB210's flying career was destined to be short. On January 12, 1952, its crew were conducting in-flight engine shutdown and relight tests. Fuel from three previously unsuccessful relights had spilled into the wing structure and caught fire. The pilot, 'Jock' Bryce, ordered the three flight test observers to bale out followed by Bryce and his co-pilot, Sqn Ldr B H D Foster, who both ejected over Holmsley South airfield at 6,000ft. Bryce and the observers survived, but Foster apparently struck the fin and was killed instantly. While the loss was a tragedy for Vickers, the aircraft had completed sufficient flight testing to convince the Air Staff all was well. The second prototype, the Type 667, serialled WB215 was only weeks away from completion and as such, the loss of WB210 did not disrupt the flight programme as much as it could have.

WB215 made its maiden flight from Wisley's new runway on April 11, 1952, powered by four Avon RA7 engines rather than the planned Sapphire turbojets.

Four different variants of the Vickers Valiant were destined to enter RAF service. These were the Type 706 (Valiant B.1), a pure bomber variant; the Type 710 (Valiant B(PR).1), another bomber variant but also with a photographic reconnaissance capability; the Type 758 (Valiant B(K).1), a bomber aircraft which could also operate as a tanker and the Type 733 (Valiant B.PR(K).1), again, a bomber variant but also with photographic reconnaissance and tanker capabilities.

RIGHT: **WJ954 was the only Valiant B.2 variant built. It made its maiden flight on September 4, 1953, from Wisley and a few days later made its first public appearance at the SBAC Farnborough air show.**

THE SOLE 'BLACK BOMBER' (TYPE 673 VALIANT B.2)

Well before the Valiant B.1 even entered service, another exciting and advanced variant of the aircraft was produced. This was the Type 673, Valiant B.2 which thanks to its high-gloss black finish (allegedly on the instructions of test pilot Brian Trubshaw) was nicknamed the 'Black Bomber'. Keen with what they saw on paper, in April 1952 the Air Ministry order 17 B.2s, made up of two prototypes and 15 operational aircraft. This version of the Valiant was designed to operate at night as a low-level pathfinder, an ironic situation as it was this very role which would bring the early demise of the aircraft in RAF service.

Destined to be the last prototype built at Foxwarren again under the watchful eye of 'Charlie' Houghton, the Valiant B.2 differed from the original design in several ways, most significantly, on the surface. The main undercarriage, which was redesigned with four main wheels, retracted rearwards into large Küchemann bodies rather than into the wing. This repositioning allowed the wing to be strengthened, especially around the now spare, wheel wells. As a result, the aircraft could comfortably withstand the considerable loads placed upon the airframe when flying at low-level and high speed.

With Gabe Robb 'Jock' Bryce in the left-hand seat and Brian Trubshaw on the right, the Valiant B.2, serialled WJ954, made its maiden flight on September 4, 1953, from Wisley and a few days later made its first public appearance at the SBAC Farnborough. WJ954 was destined to be the only Valiant B.2 built, defence cuts were already beginning to take their toll during the early 1950s before rearmament had fully taken effect. Powered by four Rolls-Royce Avon RA.14 engines, the Valiant B.2 had a maximum speed of 640mph and had great potential.

Sadly, the Air Staff had moved the requirement again and the contract for 17 Valiant B.2s was cancelled, leaving WJ954 as the sole example of the mark. The Valiant B.2 continued to fly some further trials work but was struck off charge on March 18, 1958 and was destined to further undignified service with the Proof and Experimental Establishment at Shoeburyness from July 2. Along with several other airframes, the Valiant was used to assess the vulnerability of aircraft to gunfire, although no actual live rounds were fired. Instead, the aircraft was slowly destroyed by metal rods being punched into the fuselage, these replicating warheads of Blue Jay, Red Dean and VR.725 missiles.

The Armageddon Arsenal

Tom Allett recalls *Operation Grapple*, the series of tests in the late 1950s that proved Britain's Hydrogen bomb capabilities.

ritain had built its first long-range, nuclear-capable jet bombers and delivered them to the Royal Air Force in 1953. The nation had achieved nuclear detonations in several ground-level tests, but it still needed to prove that its fledgling bomb technology and delivery methods worked in a more realistic operational environment, especially when dropped from an aircraft. Another obvious problem was that scientists from other nations – including those of a potential enemy – were clearly ahead of the British nuclear team.

The final test of *Operation Buffalo* had proved the RAF was capable of a nuclear airdrop at the first time of asking. The detonation of a Blue Danube bomb at the Kite site within the Marlalinger Test Range in Southern Australia on October 11, 1956, delivered an explosive yield of about three kilotonnes. Such force would deliver a terrible blow

to any target unfortunate enough to receive it, but by 1956 the United States and the Soviet Union were focussed upon developing an even-more terrifying threat. The Hiroshima and Nagasaki bombs were atomic weapons (A-bombs) that produced their explosive power through nuclear fission, but the weapons scientists were now focused upon honing the next-generation weapon, the Hydrogen bomb.

The H-bomb uses nuclear fission to create nuclear fusion, capable of producing a far greater destructive force. To an extent, even the relatively new Hiroshima-type bombs were about to become obsolete in any potential war between superpowers, and the British Government wanted to retain its current status as a world power.

Despite the achievements of the *Operation Buffalo* airdrop, it was obvious Britain was still trailing the USA and USSR.

WP223

CABINET DECISION

In 1954 the Cabinet, wanting to bolster its waning 'world power' status, decided it must also develop thermonuclear weapons within the British Hydrogen Bomb Programme (BHBP).

Understandably, there was some public and political opposition to the very existence of nuclear weapons of any kind. Debates in the House of Commons covered everything from whether it was even necessary for Britain to own and develop nuclear weapons through to, if the answer is yes, should live detonation tests be permitted in the Earth's atmosphere?

The USA and the USSR were already established as the world's first nuclear powers and their governments, working with the United Nations, had begun talks to negotiate an easing of the escalating arms race and provide at least a temporary halt in nuclear testing. The British Government was concerned that a proposed moratorium would impose a global test ban before Britain was established as an independent nuclear power. From now on, the time pressure to build a British H-bomb was ever-present.

Soon after becoming Prime Minister in April 1955, the new premier, Anthony Eden, spoke to the British public via a radio broadcast. He underlined why Britain needed to become a nuclear power and reaffirmed his government's determination to push ahead with the development of nuclear bombs. However, simply developing them would not be enough, they must also be tested. He explained: "You cannot prove a bomb until it has exploded. "Nobody can know whether it is effective or not until it has been tested." »

MAIN PICTURE:
This image shows a test-drop of an inert *Blue Danube* bomb, but the scene replicates the occasion of Britain's first live test drops performed in the 1950s.
(KEY Archive)

"You cannot prove a bomb until it has exploded. Nobody can know whether it is effective or not until it has been tested"
- British Prime Minister Anthony Eden, April 1955

LEFT: The runway at Christmas Island's airfield was extended to handle the RAF's Valiant jet bombers. The remote central Pacific Ocean locations of Malden Island and Christmas Island (now known as Kiritimati) were chosen as the key locations for the *Grapple* series of nuclear tests.
(KEY Archive)

Backed by the results of its early series of A-bomb tests, plans were drawn up for a series of four increasingly powerful atomic weapon tests within the BHPB. They comprised nine explosions and included both atomic and hydrogen bombs.

Many potential test sites were evaluated but the list of locations was gradually reduced to the two with most potential.

The remote central Pacific Ocean locations of Malden Island and Christmas Island (now known as Kiritimati), just north of the equator and within the chain of mid-Pacific Northern Line atolls and islands, were chosen as the key locations. Both the British and the Americans claimed them as being in their sphere of influence and neither had their own independent governments.

The bomb project was given the codename *Operation Grapple*. Christmas Island was selected as the operational base while Malden would be the detonation site.

Christmas Island had no indigenous population and was primarily covered in grass, scrubland, or coconut plantations. Situated almost 1,500 miles from Tahiti, around 1,300 miles from Hawaii, more than 3,200 miles from San Francisco and approximately 4,000 miles from Sydney, it was remote by any standards. However, that remoteness would impact upon many aspects of the preparations and the extended supply chains for *Grapple*. Some supply items took weeks to reach the islands.

Despite having no indigenous people, more than 250 civilians from the Gilbert and Ellice Islands lived on Christmas Island and were mainly employed at the coconut plantations. Most were only short-terms visitors, taking the opportunity to earn an income from the plantations before moving on to the next payday, but others had worked there for many years.

While Christmas Island was the main base, the area surrounding Malden Island some 400 miles to the south would be the drop-zone. Some 200 miles further south Penrhyn Island doubled up as a weather station and test monitoring site. It housed a United States Air Force special weapons monitoring unit, so the island's runway was lengthened, and its general infrastructure was enhanced to enable USAF Douglas C-124 Globemaster IIs transport aircraft to operate from there.

RAF COMMANDERS

Although overall command of *Grapple* was initially given to a high-ranking Royal Navy officer, he said that as it was primarily an RAF operation, the RAF should provide the Task force Commander. Air Commodore Wilfrid Oulton was duly appointed on February 6, 1956, and within a month had been given the acting rank of air vice marshal. Group Captain Richard Gething became his chief of staff and Group Captain Cecil 'Ginger' Weir was appointed as the Air Task Group Commander.

The first meeting of the Grapple Executive Committee took place in London on February 21, 1956. At the time, there were numerous domestic and international voices calling for a moratorium on nuclear testing which put the team under even greater pressure to get the bomb tests done, and April 1, 1957, was set as the start date.

PREPARATIONS

Four Vickers Valiants from 49 Squadron were allocated for the bombing tasks, although the RAF committed many more aircraft for the job. Two Canberra units – 76 and 100 squadrons – were deployed, along with the Shackletons of 206 and 240 squadrons and a flight of Westland Whirlwind helicopters from 22 Squadron were provided to cover search and rescue duties.

RAF Douglas Dakotas and Handley Page Hastings provided the inter-island transport capability.

As the Light Aircraft Carrier HMS *Warrior* was acting as the Naval Task Group Commander's flagship, it too provided aerial support in the shape of its Grumman Avengers and four Royal Navy Whirlwind helicopters along with two more from the RAF. While the former were usually attack / torpedo aircraft, they were tasked with patrol duties while the six extra helicopters boosted the search and rescue force. The first RAF personnel arrived on Christmas Island in a Shackleton on June 19, 1956, and further advance parties of personnel from the RAF and Royal Engineers arrived by ship a matter of days later. Both teams quickly began the series of airfield, port and road improvement required of them. They were supported by two construction squads from the Fiji Defence Force and several of the Gilbertese civilians who were without work ≫

LEFT: The mushroom cloud develops from Britain's first thermonuclear explosion during *Operation Grapple* on May 15, 1957.
(Public Domain)

due to the plantations' enforced closure during *Grapple*. Their combined efforts enabled Christmas Island to be declared operational on December 1, 1956, with its runway extended to accommodate the Valiants.

Extra support came from the US authorities who allowed the RAF's aircraft to overfly the USA, even when carrying radioactive or explosive equipment. The availability of such direct routing avoided the need to transit through the winter conditions that would have been experienced flying over Canada, so there was no need for them to use valuable space carrying winter survival equipment. Some RAF ground personnel were based at Hickham Air Force Base (Pearl Harbor), Hawaii, while others were accommodated at Travis AFB in California. To help uphold morale, RAF personnel were allowed to take their leave days in these 'exotic' locations.

By the end of April 1957 most of the Gilbertese workers and their families had been evacuated to Fanning Island 300 miles to the northeast of Christmas Island. They would all return three months later, rejoining the handful of Gilbertese men who had remained on Christmas Island as employees of the construction teams.

A-BOMB TO H-BOMB

Britain's Atomic Weapons Research Establishment at Aldermaston produced three designs for the *Grapple* bombs. The first, *Orange Herald*, was a boosted fission weapon, the second, *Green Bamboo*, was effectively an interim thermonuclear bomb, while the third, *Green Granite* was a true Hydrogen bomb. *Grapple* would determine their respective potential.

The initial *Grapple* series comprised three tests with all bombs to be dropped and detonated at 45,000ft over Malden Island (to reduce the level of nuclear fallout) between May and June 1957. Their high-altitude detonation made the usual barometric trigger switches unsuitable, and the explosions would be controlled by a clockwork timer instead.

The first, *Grapple 1*, required Wing Commander Ken Hubbard, flying a Vickers Valiant, to drop a remodelled version *Green Granite* known as *Short Granite*. Hubbard had been an operational bomber pilot during World War Two flying Vickers Wellingtons. Post-war he continued flying famous bomber types, including the Avro Lancaster, before having the opportunity to apply for a posting to one of the then new V-Force units. After learning to fly Meteor and Canberra jets, he had the opportunity to acquaint himself with Vickers' latest bomber – the four-jet Valiant, learning to fly it with 232 Operational Conversion Unit at RAF Gaydon, Warwickshire. He subsequently joined the newly reformed 49 Squadron as its commanding officer at RAF Wittering. The unit had eight Valiants and deployed four of them to Christmas Island: XD818 flown by the now Wing Commander Hubbard; XD822 piloted by Squadron Leader LD Roberts; XD823 flown by Squadron

The next test was *Grapple 2*, which evaluated *Orange Herald* on May 31. This time the bomb was dropped from XD822 flown by Roberts, while Steele took the controls of the grandstand aircraft, XD823.

This time the drop could have ended in disaster. The bomb was released at 1044 local time and Roberts then entered the briefed 60° banked turn to fly away from the explosion. At this critical moment the bomber's accelerometer failed leaving Roberts unable to accurately judge the gravitational 'G-Force' acceleration of his aircraft and the Valiant entered a high-speed stall. One can only image the crews' thoughts while their aircraft was temporarily out of control while in the vicinity of an imminent nuclear explosion! Thankfully, Roberts recovered the situation and escaped the danger area. The bomb detonated at 45,000ft producing an estimated explosive yield equivalent to the explosive force of 720-800 kilotonnes of TNT. At that time, it was the largest blast ever achieved by a single-stage device and from a technical point of view made it a megaton-range device. The government acclaimed it as a hydrogen bomb and hid the fact that it was actually a large fission bomb until the end of the Cold War some 34 years later. Its success did much to dispel any remaining British doubts lingering from the only partial achievement of the previous test, but there were still several hurdles to jump.

Grapple 3 was essentially used to test a series of 'fixes' for problems encountered during the first two detonations so *Purple Granite*, a derivative of the *Short Granite* bomb was used. It was dropped by Steele's crew on June 19 from XD823 as Millett's crew 'grandstanded' in XD824. The bomb delivered a yield equivalent to 'only' 200 kilotonnes of TNT, even less than achieved during *Grapple 2*. The 'fixes' had obviously not worked and the time pressure to achieve all their goals before the expected moratorium became greater than ever. Nevertheless, the next tests would take several months to prepare. The crews from 49 Squadron were able to return home for a while but many of the three-services' personnel had to stay on with the promise that their Pacific deployment would last no longer than one year. »

Leader Arthur Steele and XD824 with Squadron Leader Barney Millett at the controls. The remaining four stayed at Wittering but were used to ferry bomb components to Christmas Island as and when required.

A 500 x 600-nautical mile exclusion zone was drawn up around the islands and patrolled by Royal Navy warships assisted by RAF Shackletons. May 15 was chosen as the date for the first H-bomb drop although full-scale rehearsals were held on May 11 and May 14. Only a small working team remained on Malden Island to take to their shelters during the test while everyone else was evacuated to either a neighbouring island or one of the several observation ships anchored in the vicinity.

When the day dawned for Hubbard to enter the RAF's history books, he released his bomb just off the coast of Malden Island at 1038 local time from an altitude of 45,000ft. Sqn Ldr Millett and crew accompanied the leader in XD824 – the so-called 'grandstand' aircraft – to observe the drop. It was calculated that Hubbard's crew missed their intended target point by just over 400 yards, but this was a tiny margin of error for a bomb of such power. Its detonation was calculated to have delivered a yield of some 300 kilotonnes of TNT, which was far below its designed capability but, despite this partial failure, it was acclaimed as a successful thermonuclear explosion. However, the British government temporarily refused to confirm or deny that the nation had become the world's third thermonuclear power.

LEFT: **Wing Commander Ken Hubbard had the responsibility of dropping Britain's first live hydrogen bomb. Hubbard had been an operational bomber pilot during World War Two flying Vickers Wellingtons. Post-war he continued flying famous bomber types, including the Avro Lancaster, before having the opportunity to apply for a posting to one of the then new V-Force units.** (Public Domain)

RIGHT: The Valiants usually returned to their UK base at RAF Wittering during the long breaks between each series of tests and at that point some of the squadron's aircraft were swapped for others. Valiant XD827, prominent in this picture, did not participate in *Grapple 1*, but was deployed later and went on to drop the last live nuclear weapon released from a V-bomber. (KEY Archive)

FURTHER SERIES

Grapple's second test series took pace in November 1957, and it is fair to say that the western powers were in shock at that time following the appearance of Russia's Sputnik 1 satellite which had orbited the Earth on October 4. There was never a clearer warning that the Russians were winning the technology race, for the time being at least. Britain pushed ahead with its series of nuclear tests and *Grapple X* involved a single detonation scheduled for November 1.

This time the bomb was to be released near the southern tip of Christmas Island instead of Malden. The new drop site's proximity to Christmas Island's airfield and its near 3,000 inhabitants – approximately 20 miles away – meant another large 'Malden-style' building programme was required. A new control room was built, and 26 blast-proof shelters were provided, while observation and monitoring equipment was established on Malden and Fanning Islands. At about 0100hrs, just as the Valiant crews were preparing for take-off, a patrolling RAF Shackleton reported sighting a ship entering the exclusion zone. It was identified as the SS *Effie*, sailing under a Liberian flag. Several other ships, mainly fishing boats, had been shepherded away on previous days but the exclusion zone Notice to Mariners had only been issued after the *Effie* had left its last port of call, and so had not seen the warning. The Shackleton circled the *Effie* while trying to make radio contact – initially in vain – so the Royal Navy destroyer *Cossack* was sent to intercept the errant vessel. This caused a significant take-off delay at the airfield, but the Shackleton's crew eventually established radio contact and the *Effie* turned about to exit the danger zone. This was transmitted back

BELOW: Vickers Valiant XD818 dropped Britain's first hydrogen bomb during the *Grapple 1* trial at Christmas Island (now Kiritimati). (Andrew Hay/flyingart.co.uk)

to the operation's HQ at about 0615 and the Valiant crews were able to take-off at 0735. Sqn Ldr Millett led in XD824 with Flt Lt Bates following in the grandstand aircraft '825. They were already manoeuvring towards the drop site when *Cossack* reported the *Effie* had left the exclusion zone and *Grapple X* was released from 45,000ft at 0847. This time the yield of 1.8 megatonnes of TNT was far greater than the 1 megatonne predicted by the scientists and some of *Cossack*'s crew later reported the shock of the blast they felt, even though they were prepared for it. Even when shielding their eyes some reported that the explosion "outshone the sun" on that blue-sky day. Some of Christmas Island's new buildings and equipment were also damaged by the fiercer than expected blast.

Although most of *Grapple X*'s explosive power was created by a thermonuclear reaction rather than nuclear fission, it was still a true hydrogen bomb. Despite having consumed a significant amount of the country's stock of highly enriched – and hugely expensive – uranium, it confirmed Britain's H-bomb status beyond any doubt.

MOST POWERFUL

Despite the success of '*X*' even greater explosive power was generated during the third test series in April 1958 when *Grapple Y* was dropped at 1005 local time on April 28, 1958, from a Valiant flown by Sqn Ldr Robert Bates. The weapon's design meant that most of its explosive power was created through thermonuclear fusion rather than fission, making the internal reaction much more efficient – and deadly. It produced an explosive yield of approximately three megatonnes of TNT, setting a record that still

stands for the most powerful British nuclear weapon ever tested. However, *Grapple Y* proved to be much more than just the 'biggest bang'. It was a major milestone along Britain's path to being a first-rate nuclear power because its fusion of heavy uranium – the raw material surrounding the explosive core that holds the detonation reaction 'together' – made the explosive process far more efficient. More importantly, its explosive yield had been accurately predicted and that proved the scientists fully understood the most efficient detonation procedure.

Even though there was much jubilation amongst the programme's physicists, there was still a closing series of four tests to complete and, once again, time was of the essence. On August 22, 1958, US President and wartime hero, Dwight D Eisenhower, announced an agreement had been made upon the much-discussed world-wide moratorium on nuclear testing. It would start on October 31 that year and run for 12 months. Britain effectively had two months to either complete *Grapple Z* or face the prospect of having permanently unfinished business, but the nation had commenced *Grapple Z* that same day. Britain was not alone in its desire to continue testing and the US, USSR and Britain all made a determined effort to complete as many detonations as possible before the deadline was reached. *Grapple Z* was designed to explore the opportunities to further boost the weapons' efficiency while making them invulnerable to the possibility of predetonation in the event of other nuclear explosions taking place near them. As the early plutonium bombs were deemed to be particularly vulnerable to predetonation the topic was treated as Most Secret to hide the fact that Britain's nuclear arsenal was vulnerable to being eliminated in that way.

Prior to the moratorium announcement, the British government had only approved two more nuclear tests, set for August 15 and September 1 but the physicists wanted four. Again, four of 49 Squadron's Valiants, XD818, XD822, XD824 and XD827, were deployed to Christmas Island. All were in place by July 31. However, despite the presence of the state-of-the-art jet bombers, another release method was about to be introduced. The first *Grapple Z* test, a fission bomb codenamed *Pendant*, could not fit into an air-droppable casing so it was suspended from four barrage balloons. The technique had been tried before during the 1957 bomb tests in Australia but had potentially huge safety drawbacks such as what do you do if the balloons break free of their moorings with a live atomic bomb attached? Strangely, there was an unexpected delay caused by the loss of the bomb's firing harness. While being delivered to Christmas Island by air it was 'lost' – or stolen

– while transiting through San Francisco International Airport and a replacement had to be sent. The bomb's nuclear core arrived on August 12 and, ten days later, *Pendant* was lifted to 1,500ft and detonated over the southeast corner of the island at 0900. Its explosive yield was estimated to be equal to 24 kilotonnes of TNT.

The delivery of the second weapon, codenamed *Flagpole*, was the responsibility of the Valiant crews. It was dropped at 0824 on September 2 by Squadron Leader Bill Bailey's crew flying XD822 with Flt Lt Tiff O'Connor's XD818 on 'grandstand' duties. It was the first time that a live British nuclear bomb had been released 'blind' – aiming by radar instead of a visual bombsight – a method that would usually be employed when a target is covered by cloud. The crew of '822 was assessed as having placed the bomb within 95yds of the aiming point when it detonated at 8,500ft – an outstanding result under the circumstances – creating an explosive force equivalent to 1.2 megatonnes of TNT.

The penultimate *Grapple* test involved a quite different design that used a three-stage explosion. Codenamed *Halliard* it had two fission mechanisms followed by a third thermonuclear element that was designed to be invulnerable to predetonation caused by other nuclear explosions. Following the techniques' earlier success, *Halliard* would also be dropped by Blind radar bombing, although the crews involved recognised there was little chance of achieving the same accuracy as before.

LEFT: **Given its historic status, XD818 thankfully escaped the scrapman's axe and is now the sole surviving complete example of a Vickers Valiant. Today it is owned by the Royal Air Force Museum and is seen here during its time at Hendon. It now resides at the RAF Cosford museum.** (KEY Archive)

There was concern about the potential dangers of dropping a live H-bomb through cloud when the average accuracy error of such drops was 215 metres and there was no way of checking if the targeting instruments were calibrated correctly. Nevertheless, the task fell to Flt Lt O'Connor in XD827, accompanied by Sqn Ldr Tony Calliard 'grandstanding'. At 0715 on September 11, 1958, O'Connor roared down the runway with Calliard close behind. As they made their way to the target area the ground radar transmitter failed, and O'Connor was authorised to perform a visual drop. At 0849 *Halliard* exploded at an altitude of 8,500ft and a recorded distance of 240m from the target. Its yield, estimated to be around 800 kilotonnes, was close to the physicists' predictions and therefore deemed to be a satisfactory result. Although its significance was only realised later, *Halliard*, released from XD827, thankfully proved to be the last live nuclear weapon dropped from a V-bomber. The final *Grapple* test, that of the codename *Burgee* bomb, used barrage balloons as the release method on September 23, 1958.

Britain's bomb physicists and engineers had proven they had the knowledge to produce reliable nuclear weapons and the Royal Air Force had proven it had an aircraft capable of delivering them.

Just a month after *Grapple Z* was concluded, the year-long moratorium on nuclear testing came into force. It was subsequently extended, and Britain has never recommenced atmospheric nuclear testing.

XD818

There was much kudos to be gained from a posting to an RAF Valiant unit in the late 1950s. Despite being a far more conventional design than the Victor and Vulcan that followed it, it was still a state-of the-art machine that reached operational ceilings beyond that of many contemporary fighters. It was also the first home-grown type to take responsibility for Britain's nuclear deterrent, the ultimate 'hush-hush' task in the British forces. One former-Valiant pilot told me that during his training he converted directly from the single propellor-engined Piston Provost to the four-jet V-bomber, which was about three times the size of the basic training aircraft he had just left. He recalled how it took him some time to get used to sitting so high up in the air compared to the Provost and that landings were additionally tricky because he was several feet higher from the ground than he was used to.

Of course, the Vickers Valiant earned its place in RAF history by dropping Britain's first live hydrogen bomb, (see page 16) but it was also the first jet-powered 'heavy' bomber. »

Highs and Lows

Tom Allett studies the key points of
the Valiant's RAF service.

RIGHT: The Vickers Valiant once held the record for a long-distance flight. The aircraft was XD861 which was used extensively by 214 Sqn before being struck off charge in March 1965, when the unit surrendered its Valiants to be reformed in July the following year with Handley Page Victors. (KEY Archive)

BELOW: A Flight Refuelling Mk 16 Hose Drum Unit (HDU) is prepared for fitting in Vickers Valiant XD861. One of the groundcrew holds the Mk 9 drogue, which had taken a great deal of trial and error to perfect, eventually having distinctive longitudinal slots cut into the surface of the cone. (KEY Archive)

SERVICE LIFE

The first outfit to be equipped with the Valiant was 139 Squadron after forming at RAF Gaydon on January 1, 1955. Shortly afterward, 232 Operational Conversion Unit (OCU), tasked with training crews for the new jet formed on February 21. As the type was realistically part of a completely new class of bombers, in the early months of operation only experienced crews were selected to fly it and 1,750 flying hours was the minimum experience required for the aircraft's captains. They must also have completed at least one tour on the Canberra medium bomber jet while co-pilots required 700hrs to qualify. The three other crew members had to have been recommended by their respective commanding officers to be considered for the Valiant. A Canberra OCU was also based at Gaydon to help facilitate crews transferring between the two types.

At its peak, the Valiant equipped ten RAF Squadrons and was deemed to have performed extremely well during the annual bombing competition hosted by the United States Air Force's Strategic Air Command.

As detailed previously, on October 11, 1956, Valiant B.1, WZ366, from 49 Squadron, flown by Edwin Flavell, became the first British aircraft to drop an atomic bomb which was released at an Australian test site. Windscreen blinds were fitted inside the cockpit for the event to help protect its crew from the intense nuclear flash and, on landing the airframe was checked over for potential damage and radioactive contamination. The following year, on May 15, 1957, pilot Ken Hubbard took Britain into the hydrogen bomb 'club' while flying XD818.

SUEZ

In between those two red letter nuclear dates, in November 1956, four RAF Valiant units - 138, 148, 207, and 214 squadrons - took part in *Operation Musketeer*, the ill-fated invasion of Egypt known as the Suez crisis. Operating from Luqa, Malta the type was so new to service that the RAF crews were still developing their bombing techniques and the Valiants were primarily to be used in the high-altitude reconnaissance role. Nevertheless, the Valiant became the first V-bomber to experience combat when used to bomb several key Egyptian targets - airfields, radio stations and transport centres. On the first night of *Musketeer*, six Valiants were sent to attack Cairo West Air Base, but the raid

was aborted in-flight due to a potential risk to American personnel nearby. Six more Valiants bombed the Almaza Air Base while a further five attacked Kibrit Airbase and Huckstep Barracks.

Even though Egyptian forces did not attempt to fight back and no Valiants were lost, the RAF thought the results disappointing. The Valiants were recorded as having dropped 842 tons of bombs although only three of their seven designated targets were judged to be seriously damaged. It would be almost 27 years before another V-bomber was in combat, during the Falklands War of 1982 (see page 94).

SAMS CHANGE EVERYTHING

In 1960, when the shooting down of Gary Powers' Lockheed U-2 spy plane underlined the fact that even ultra-high-flying aircraft were vulnerable to the new generation of surface-to-air missiles, the original high-level bombing role was dropped. The crews retrained for low-level penetration techniques and the white anti-flash colour schemes were replaced by grey/green camouflage and by 1963 four squadrons, 49,148, 207, and 214, had been transferred to fly under the control of Supreme Allied Commander Europe (SACEUR) in the low-level tactical bombing role. At this point their peacetime duties revolved around maintaining their operational efficiency. This primarily involved dropping practise bombs on instrumented bombing ranges where a procedure using radio tones to mark the point of the bomb drop allowed the bomb error to be deduced by a ground radar unit and passed to headquarters for analysis and the flight crew while they were still airborne. Most of the bomber pilots were ex-World War Two veterans and their experience combined with the Valiant's Navigational and Bombing system (NBS) usually enabled good results to be obtained, even from 45,000ft in daylight. »

BELOW: **Vickers Valiant of 53 Squadron taking off from Luqa, Malta during Exercise** *Medflex*. **The exercise was part training operation and part muscle-flexing show of force in the unsettled North African and Middle East regions. In addition to the combined air, land and sea exercises, a mushroom cloud burst simulated an atomic explosion. It was designed to demonstrate the military preparedness of the 'the peoples allied for peace' under the North Atlantic Treaty Organisation (NATO) umbrella.** (KEY Archive)

RIGHT: **In 1963 a squadron of Javelin fighters, refuelled by Valiant tankers, were able to fly to India in stages to take part in Exercise** *Shiksha*, **supporting Indian forces during a border dispute with China.**
(KEY Archive)

AIR-TO-AIR REFUELLING

Two Valiant squadrons, 214 at Marham and 90 at Honington flew the tanker variant aircraft on a limited basis from 1958 and '59 respectively until becoming full-time tanker units on April 1, 1962. All aircraft assigned to the tanker role were fitted with a Hose Drum Unit (HDU) in the bomb bay. It was attached to bomb mounting points so that it could be removed easily if required but this meant that the aircraft's bomb doors had to be opened every time it needed to give fuel to a receiver aircraft.

The HDU was operated via a control panel at the radar navigator's position and the HDU could be quickly removed if the aircraft was required to revert to its bombing role. As in-flight refuelling probes were fitted to all V-bombers, they all had extended range and the RAF performed several long-range demonstration flights using Valiant tankers deployed along a planned route in advance.

In 1960 a Valiant flew non-stop from its base at RAF Marham to Singapore and just a year later a Vulcan flew non-stop from Britain to Australia with the help of Valiant tanker support which had themselves performed non-stop flights from the UK to Nairobi, Kenya, RAF Gan in the Maldives, and Singapore.

In 1963 a squadron of Javelin fighters were refuelled by Valiant tankers enabling them to fly to India in stages to take part in Exercise *Shiksha*, supporting Indian forces during a border dispute with China. Other aircraft types supported by Valiant tankers included Victors, Vulcans, English Electric Lightnings, and Royal Navy de Havilland Sea Vixens and Supermarine Scimitars.

COUNTERMEASURES ARE RECONNAISSANCE

The Valiants of 18 Squadron at RAF Finningley were modified to undertake radio countermeasures (RCM) tasks – now known as electronic countermeasures (ECM) – which required jamming transmitters to be fitted. Little is known about their highly secretive work, but seven aircraft were converted. Over at RAF Wyton, 543 Squadron Valiants were converted to the photo-reconnaissance role. Perhaps their most public task was to photograph 400,000sq miles of Rhodesia during an eleven-week tasking in 1965.

FATIGUE AND RETIREMENT

In 1956 Vickers conducted a series of low altitude test flights in WZ383 to assess the Valiant for low-level flights at high speed. The manufacturer determined that several modifications were needed including the fitting of a metal radome, debris guards on the two inboard engines and after six test flights the aileron and elevator artificial 'feel' was reduced by 50% but pilots still reported problems with condensation and the aircraft's cabin heating system. Data recording equipment was fitted which gathered information that would be used to determine how much longer the aircraft could fly safely for at low-level. Initially a figure of 75 hours was calculated but that was subsequently changed to 'fewer than 200'. The number of annual flying hours carried out by each airframe was suddenly becoming an issue for the RAF and the Royal Aircraft Establishment (RAE) then ran a similar run of tests that were more representative of operational flying conditions. Its report, published in 1958, contained information about which flight conditions caused the most damage and enabled a better projection of the Valiant's future operational life. However, in July 1964, a cracked wing spar was found on an operational aircraft and that August the failure of a starboard wing rear spar in WP217 at 30,000ft led to the crew being forced to make a flapless – though successful – landing back at Gaydon. An inspection revealed that the

LEFT: RAF Gaydon was home to Valiant and Canberra Operational Conversion Units at the same time. This image was taken in 1956. (KEY Archive)

fuselage skin below the artboard inner plane had buckled, popping the rivets. Other cracks and pulled rivets were found near the engines and the top surface of the skin on the wing between two engines had buckled. Both aircraft involved were photo-reconnaissance versions.

Fleet-wide inspections were called for and revealed wing spars were suffering from metal fatigue at between 35% and 75% of the assessed safe fatigue life. It was thought that this was probably due to the turbulence encountered by the aircraft when flying at low-level. Following the findings, the aircraft were divided into three categories: Cat A – aircraft continuing to fly; Cat B – must fly to a repair base; and Cat C – require repair before flying again. The tanker units were found to have the highest number of Cat A machines because they normally operated at high-altitude.

The number of airframes gathering at RAF Maintenance Units began to rise and they were designated as 'non-effective aircraft.'

Initially there was no suggestion of retiring the Valiant fleet or even most of the effected airframes. Repairs continued at RAF bases but in January 1965 the government decided the repairs were too expensive to continue with and the entire fleet was grounded on January 26. The honour of performing the last Valiant tanker sortie – albeit unknown at the time – fell to XD812 of 214 Squadron which was refuelling Lightings over the North Sea on December 9, 1964, when its crew were instructed to land back at Marham before the planned exercise was complete. That same day, the last bomber Valiant flight was performed by XD818.

BELOW: A bomber variant from 214 Squadron. This unit later converted to the Victor. (KEY Archive)

Valiant
Walkaround

The Valiant was the first of the Royal Air Force's V-Bomber types and was used to establish the UK's nuclear deterrent, releasing Britain's first air-dropped atomic and hydrogen bombs. This meant that a single Valiant had more destructive power than one of the 1,000-bomber raids performed by the RAF in World War Two. The Valiant had no defensive armament and relied on the speed and altitude attained from its four turbojet engines and state-of-the-art electronic countermeasures to survive in hostile Eastern Bloc airspace.

Cosford's B.1 XD818 is the last surviving complete Valiant and resides within the museum's Cold War exhibition alongside its V-force family members.

Data:	Valiant B.1
Length:	108ft 3in (32.99m)
Wingspan:	114ft 4in (34.84m)
Height:	32ft 2in (9.8m)
Wing Area:	2,362sq ft (219.43m²)
Cruising speed:	Mach 0.75
Maximum speed:	Mach 0.84
Range:	4,500nm (8,334km)
Service ceiling:	54,000ft (16,459m)
Engines:	4 x Rolls-Royce Avon RA.28s

MAIN PICTURE:
Given its role in the development of Britain's nuclear deterrent, Vickers Valiant XD818 must surely rank as one of the RAF's most important airframes of all time.
(RAF Museum Cosford)

RIGHT: One huge 1,615 imp gal fuel tank was a permanent fixture under each wing. These provided fuel to their own aircraft while tanker variants had fuel tanks fitted within their bomb bay to enable them to feed recipient aircraft. (Tom Allett)

RIGHT: The Avon was Rolls-Royce's first axial-flow powerplant design and proved to be an enormous success, powering several different aircraft types. (Tom Allett)

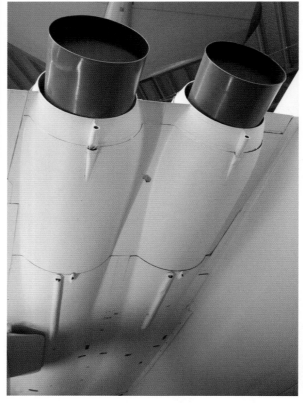

RIGHT: Many elements of the Valiant's design – including its tail – were 'conventional' compared to those of its V-bomber siblings. This was a decisive factor in making the aircraft ready for service before any of its rivals. (Tom Allett)

ABOVE: Again, the Valiant's relatively conventional design is illustrated by its use of just two mainwheels on either side of the fuselage, while its sister V-bombers had eight on each side. (Tom Allett)

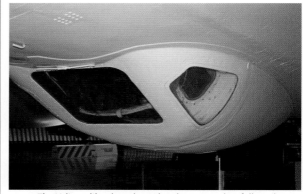

ABOVE: The Valiant, like the other V-bomber types that followed, was equipped with downward-facing windows for its bomb-aimer. A throwback design from World War Two, it was rarely used by its crews. (Tom Allett)

ABOVE: Note the heavy cockpit framing required for an aircraft of the 1950s that would be operating at what was then extreme altitude. Note also the 'eyebrow' widows at the top which afforded the pilots a better view to their left or right when the aircraft was in a steeply banked attitude. (Tom Allett)

LEFT: In this view the Valiant's crew entrance door has been removed to give a glimpse into the rear crew compartment, but its circular design illustrates how Vickers attempted to reduce the possibility of metal fatigue by removing sharp corners wherever possible. (Tom Allett)

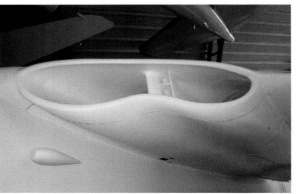

FAR LEFT: The port-wing root and air intakes that fed the Rolls-Royce Avon engines. (Tom Allett)

NEAR LEFT: In keeping with its all-white anti-nuclear flash colour scheme, XD818 wears the appropriate low-visibility markings that were applied during the 1950s and '60s. (Tom Allett)

WJ954

IN PROFILE

The Valiant

ONLY ONE Valiant B.2, WJ954, was produced. It first flew in September 1953 and its all-black colour scheme quickly led it to be known as the Black Bomber.

The B.2 was essentially a beefed-up version of the original, having a strengthened airframe and wings plus a slightly longer fuselage and new-design undercarriage that retracted backwards into wing-mounted fairings.

The British Government ordered 17 B.2s, but they were never built. Ironically, the Valiant B.1s were forced into early retirement due to the metal fatigue problems associated with low-level flying.

Had the B.2 been produced, its tougher airframe may have withstood the rigours of low-altitude operations and kept the type in service for many more years.

All profile drawings by
Andrew Hay / flyingart.co.uk

The Valiant in Miniature

Airfix produce plastic injection kits of all three V-bomber types in 1:72 scale. This superb example – built by Tony O'Toole – depicts Mk.B.1, XD857. It was one of the eight specially modified Valiant airframes that took part in Operation *Grapple*, the British hydrogen bomb tests of 1957.

Delivered to RAF Wittering on February 1, 1957, she spent her entire operational career with 49 Squadron before being struck off charge on February 19, 1965. The bomber was subsequently scrapped, but the battered remains of its cockpit section survive.

Airfix's Valiant kit was reissued in 2021 and can be built in either the markings of an all-silver B(PR)K.1, WZ393, of 90 Squadron based at RAF Honington, Suffolk, in 1957, or another all-white *Grapple* machine, XD818. (AMW – Tony O'Toole)

The Big Crescent Bird

The Handley Page HP.80 Victor was third and final V-bomber to enter service and went on to be the last to leave.
By William Noble

ABOVE: Victor prototype WB771 in flight taken by Charles Brown before the SBAC Farnborough show in July 1953. It crashed in 1954 due to tailplane flutter. (KEY Archive)

Designed under the watchful eyes of Reginald Spencer Stafford and Geoffrey Henry Lee, the Handley Page HP.80, just like the Avro Type 698 Vulcan, were deemed as being far too 'radical' to warrant an order for prototype aircraft. Sir Frederick Handley Page, the company's defiantly independent leader and the Air Staff, were in equal agreement that the bomber, which met Specification B.35/46, would require a protracted period of research before reaching the flight stage. A 1947 wind model of the original version of the HP.80 was a dramatic looking machine, featuring the crescent shaped wing, complete with large up-turned tip rudders and a tiny fin with an all-moving slab tailplane, the latter only serving as a trimmer. The fuselage had a round cross section and the four turbojet engines, were fully enclosed with the wing.

While the basics of the HP.80 were evident in the wind tunnel model, Handley Page's aerodynamicist Dr Gustav Lachmann, changed the design to a slightly more conventional looking aircraft. The fin was enlarged to improve longitudinal stability, complete with a rudder and the tailplane perched on top. This redesign made the dramatic looking wingtip control surfaces surplus to requirement, and they were removed.

THE HP.88

In 1948 it was decided that a 40% scale research aircraft should be built with a crescent-shaped wing and high T-tail arrangement as per the HP.80. Designated the HP.88 (to Specification E.6/48), the aircraft was built by Blackburn at Brough and consisted of a Supermarine Swift fuselage, fitted with a 40ft span wing that was designed with three progressive stages of sweepback of 48.5° inboard, 37.5° semi-span and 26.75° at the outboard section. A small, one-piece, all-moving tailplane was fitted on top of a swept fin and rudder, while power was provided by a 5,500lb Rolls-Royce Nene 3 turbojet.

Serialled VX330, by the time the HP.88 made its maiden flight from Carnaby in the hands of Flt Lt G R I Parker on June 21, 1951, the aircraft represented little of what the HP.80 had already become. It did, however, confirm all the wind tunnel data gathered up to this point, but the aircraft's life was destined to be very short. Just 36 days after its maiden flight, the HP.88 broke up over Stansted during a low high-speed pass, killing the pilot, Douglas Broomfield instantly.

THE PROTOTYPES

By the time of the loss of the HP.88, the first of two prototypes, serialled WB771 and WB775, was progressing well. Ordered on April 26, 1948, power was initially to be provided by four 6,800lb-thrust Metrovick F.9 axial flow turbojets which had been used in the original design laid out in 1947. By 1948, the development of Metrovick had been taken over by Armstrong Siddeley and the engine had been renamed Sapphire. By the time it was installed in WB771, the thrust had been bolstered to 7,500lb. Just like the Valiant and Vulcan, the engines were mounted in pairs, fully enclosed, and neatly installed within the wing roots.

Now named the HP.80 Victor, the wing of the aircraft increased in complexity with the installation of Fowler trailing-edge flaps, Krüger nose flaps and elevons, and speed brakes. All these features would combine to provide excellent low speed handling qualities with an aircraft that was destined to be the largest load carrier and marginally the quickest of the three V-bombers.

Regarding the load, the Victor was designed with a huge bomb bay, in part due to the lack of knowledge at the time as to how large the nuclear weapon would be. Therefore, the design of the bay was based around the ability to carry a single 22,000lb Grand Slam-type, a pair of 12,000lb Tallboy-type or, even more impressively, 35 1,000lb GP bombs, all with room to spare! Eventually the Handley Page designers were informed that the nuclear weapon would be around the 10,000lb mark. Armed with this information the designers created an arrangement based on a scaled-down *Tallboy* and created a bomb bay capable of carrying four nuclear weapons. There was an exception, the bulky, 24ft-long '*Blue Danube*' of which only one could be carried because of its dimensions. In the event of a very high weight take-off, provision was made for the installation of a pair of 8,000lb de Havilland Spectre rockets under the inner wing, which, once expended, could be jettisoned.

The Victor was equipped with a H2S Mk.9 scanner, along with a range of other avionics that were housed in a large chin blister located under the nose of the aircraft. Above this was the crew's pressurised cabin, which comprised pilot, co-pilot, tactical navigator, radar operator and electronics operator. Just like the other V-bombers, only the pilots were equipped with ejector seats, but there was at least one serious investigation into how to protect the crew which was an Air Ministry concern. Suggested by the Air Ministry, Handley Page were instructed to look at the feasibility of an escape pod which could be explosively detached from the rest of the aircraft and descend by parachute, in the event of a catastrophic emergency. Unfortunately, Handley Page ruled out the idea as it would prove to be too great a weight penalty that would significantly reduce the performance of the aircraft.

ON THE ROAD TO WILTSHIRE

WB771 was completed at Cricklewood on May 24, 1952, the plan being for the aircraft to be transported by road to Boscombe Down. At Boscombe, the MoS (Ministry of Supply) had constructed a new hangar for the HP.80 where, 60 Handley Page employees would re-assemble the aircraft for its maiden flight.

The route to Boscombe had been carefully planned, and at least two road junctions had to 'modified' with the aid of a bulldozer so that the oversize load could pass. Mounted tail-first on a tractor-powered articulated unit, the fuselage was concealed by a white canvas sheet with the words 'GELEYPANDHY-SOUTHAMPTON' stencilled upon it. The first word was meant to be an anagram of Handley Page, although the signwriter inadvertently added an extra 'Y' instead of 'A'! The journey initially progressed well, with a rest stop close to the Great West Road. Continuing along the A303 towards Andover, one of the 'modified' junctions was reached only to discover that the bulldozer was broken down, blocking the route. The bulldozer refused to start, and only after shovels were used to clear another route did the large load manage to squeeze past and reach Boscombe safely. »

RIGHT:
The HP.88 development aircraft, VX330, had only completed 14 hours of flight before it broke up in mid-air over Stansted killing its pilot, Douglas Broomfield.
(KEY Archive)

Re-assembly began almost immediately, and the plan was to get WB771 into the air for September's SBAC airshow at Farnborough. However, this was not to be, as it was discovered, thanks to that lack of a radar scanner under the forward fuselage, that the centre of gravity was too far aft. To rectify this, half a ton of scrap iron plates were bolted into the empty bay and to resolve the problem completely, all subsequent production aircraft had their forward fuselages extended by 40in. On top of this problem, further delays were incurred after a fire broke out in the rear fuselage after a system test of the hydraulic system. Three fitters were sprayed with burning hydraulic fluid during the escape from the aircraft, one of them dying in hospital 16 days later.

In the meantime, Handley Page's chief test pilot, Sqn Ldr Hedley George 'Hazel' Hazelden, who was appointed by the company in 1947, began to familiarise himself with the operation of the Sapphire turbojet engine. A pair of these powerplants had been installed, in place of the outboard piston Hercules, on the second prototype Handley Page Hastings, TE583, a configuration Hazelden had been handling since November 1950. He had become proficient enough to fly the Hastings on a single Sapphire at 170kt and gained further experience flying the Sapphire-powered Canberra B.2.

INTO THE AIR

It was a week before Christmas 1952 that Hazelden finally got to fly the prototype HP.80 Victor, WB771. The weather was atrocious, but this did not stop Hazelden from taxiing WB770 from the re-assembly hangar to the compass-swing base and back, the aircraft reportedly handling very well despite the conditions. The weather did not relent, but two days later the aircraft was fast taxied along Boscombe's main 10,000ft runway, again without issues. The weather yielded on December 24, the sky was clear, and the wind had dropped to a breeze which conveniently directed itself straight down the runway. Accompanied by flight test observer, Ian Bennett, Hazelden taxied WB771 to the end of the runway and with little fuss, opened the throttles and took to the air. After a short flight, complete with a deliberate overshoot before landing, 17 minutes later WB771 was taxiing back to the Handley Page shed.

Flight testing continued from Boscombe for two more months while the runway at Radlett was extended to accommodate the aircraft safely. The flight programme progressed well until the fourth flight on February 9, 1953. During this flight, the undercarriage was extended and retracted several times to measure the amount of buffet caused. All appeared to go well with the test, until on touchdown, all 16 mainwheel tyres burst at once. The problem was quickly found to be the arrangement for interlocking the parking brake and retraction system which stopped the wheels from spinning as they entered the undercarriage bay; the system was quickly modified, and no such problem happened again.

Not long before WB771 departed Boscombe Down, the aircraft overflew the Handley Page factory at Cricklewood and the company airfield at Radlett, to show off the aircraft to the workforce, something they would surely have been immensely proud of being part of. Hazelden delivered WB771 to Radlett for the first time on February 25, 1953. Flight testing continued unabated, the only wobbly moment occurring in April when the port undercarriage bogie became jammed in the vertical position, but Hazelden coolly managed the situation, landing the large aircraft delicately on its four rear tyres without further damage.

WB771 made its first official public appearance during the flypast at the Queen's Coronation Review at Odiham on July 5, 1953. The wider public would see the aircraft at that year's SBAC Farnborough show. For that important occasion, the aircraft's fuselage and fin was painted (up to this point the aircraft was in natural metal) matt black complete with a red cheat line and the wings and tail surfaces were finished in silver-grey. Hazelden's flying display at the show was even more impressive when it was later discovered that he carried it out with just three serviceable engines: a rogue igniter plug proving to be the problem.

RIGHT: **Remarkably, the second prototype aircraft, WB775, appeared at the 1954 SBAC Farnborough during its maiden flight.** (KEY Archive)

PUSHING THE ENVELOPE

Stage by stage, Hazelden continued to push the flight envelope of the HP.80, achieving a ceiling of 50,000ft on October 15, 1953, without experiencing any buffet at all. The next day Mach 0.83 (636mph) was reached at 47,000ft and the following day, Handley Page Deputy Test Pilot, K W Dalton-Golding took the aircraft to Mach 0.88 (675mph) at 47,500ft. Hazelden pushed the envelope even further a few days later, reaching Mach 0.91 (698mph) at 47,500ft. After further modifications, Hazelden raised the bar to Mach 0.925 (710mph) at 45,000ft, the aircraft presenting no compressibility effects and steep turns were conducted at Mach 0.88, again free of buffet. Newly appointed deputy test pilot John Allam quickly got to grips with WB771 and in February 1954 he – accidently – almost broke the sound barrier, taking the big bomber to Mach 0.98 (751mph), buckling the tailplane as a result. The second prototype, WB775, was nearing completion and rather than initiating a repair, the tailplane was borrowed and installed on WB771. The first prototype was back in the air again on June 14, when Hazelden flew it at an all-up weight of 99,000lb.

Destiny played its part for Hazelden on July 14, 1954, when, as part of his duties as Handley Page's chief test pilot, he was called away from the HP.80 trials to promote the HPR.1 Marathon – a four-engined passenger aircraft – at Woodley. Another new arrival, Ronald 'Taffy'

Ecclestone, a replacement for Dalton-Golding, (who, along with flight test observer M G Goodbridge had been killed in a Canberra crash at Radlett on February 25), would temporarily take over flight testing of the HP.80.

Tasked with conducting several, low-level calibration runs over Cranfield, all seemed well after several passes over the Bedfordshire airfield. Whilst during the final run at a mere 100ft, the tailplane began to break up and detach from the top of the fin. WB771 pitched down slightly and smashed into the runway at high speed. The crew, Ecclestone DFC and flight test observers, Ian Bennett, Bruce Heithersay and Albert Cook stood no chance. Held on by three substantial bolts, the cause of the crash was found to be metal fatigue around them and as such the tailplane was modified to be held on by four bolts instead, the problem, thankfully never rearing its head again.

The second HP.80 Victor prototype, WB775 was completed as quickly as possible and on September 11, 1954, conducted a 57-minute maiden flight from Radlett. This flight meant that it could scrape into the SBAC at Farnborough, making a flypast that same afternoon. WB775 would go on to shoulder all the preliminary Victor flight programme and perform all of the necessary trials to prepare the aircraft for operational service. An initial order for 25 Victor B.1s was placed in June 1952 and the first of these, XA917 first flew from Radlett on February 1, 1956.

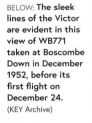

BELOW: **The sleek lines of the Victor are evident in this view of WB771 taken at Boscombe Down in December 1952, before its first flight on December 24.** (KEY Archive)

O f the 35 years' service the Handley Page Victor gave the Royal Air Force, it is quite easy for some to overlook the initial period of approximately ten years in which the aircraft operated in its intended role as a bomber – a conventional and a nuclear one. From its entry into service in 1958 as the B.1, culminating in 1968 as the B.2, the aircraft, along with the Valiant at first, and the Vulcan, played its part well as one of the trio of the V-bomber force, aka, the 'Medium Bomber Force', Bomber Command.

COTTESMORE WING

The honour of being the first operational Handley Page Victor unit was given to 10 Squadron, which was initially formed on January 1, 1915 at Farnborough. Disbanded between December 31, 1919 and January 3, 1928, the unit reformed as a bomber squadron with the Handley Page Hyderabad, progressing with the Hinaidi, Virginia, Heyford, Whitley, and Halifax before a change of role to the Dakota from May 1945, on and off until February 1950. Briefly reformed with the Canberra at Scampton and Honington from January 1953 to January 1957, the unit was disbanded again in preparation for its new, nuclear role.

Under the command of Wing Commander C B Owen DSO, DFC, AFC, 10 Squadron was reformed at Cottesmore on April 15, 1958, equipped with an establishment of eight Handley Page Victor B.1 aircraft. All aircraft were collected direct from the manufacturer at Radlett, the first being XA935, which, as you would expect

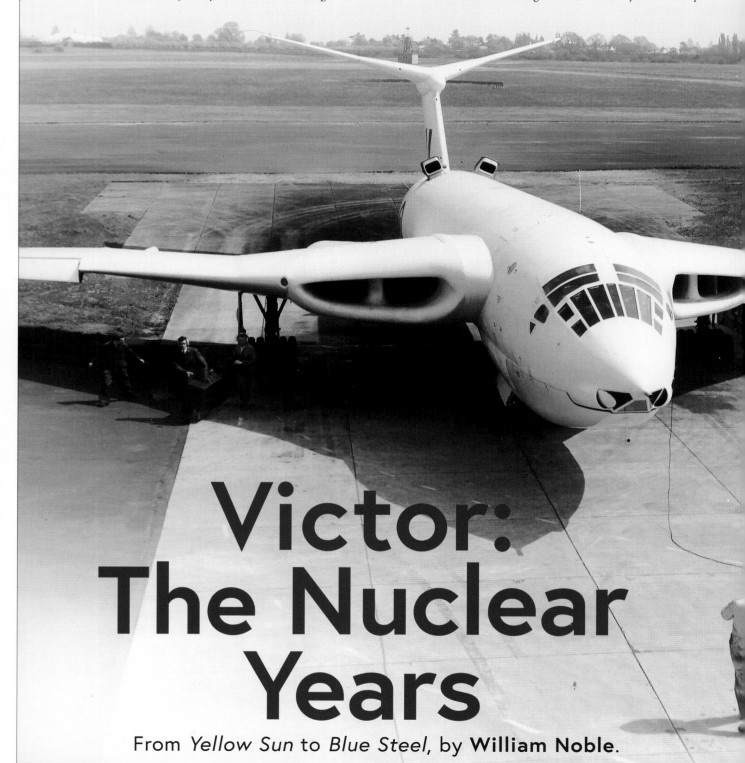

Victor: The Nuclear Years

From *Yellow Sun* to *Blue Steel,* by **William Noble.**

made the short flight from Hertfordshire to Cottesmore with the boss, Wg Cdr Owen, at the controls. Cottesmore, whose station commander was World War Two fighter 'ace', Group Captain J E 'Johnnie' Johnson, was originally earmarked for the Vickers Valiant. Johnson had already completed a course at 232 OCU at RAF Gaydon to fly the Valiant only to have to return to do the same for the Victor. Cottesmore was one of ten airfields, rebuilt to Class 1 standard for the V-Force complete with a 9,000ft runway, bolstered to take aircraft of up to 200,000lb in weight, new hardstanding's for 16 aircraft (complete with fire hydrants, electrical supply, and comms), up to date airfield lighting and landing aids plus new technical and domestic infrastructure.

HONING THE FORCE

While 10 Squadron quickly made themselves comfortable with their new aircraft and modern infrastructure, it became clear that there was no real plan as to how the Victor force would proceed should the 'balloon go up'. At this early stage, the crews were literally left to themselves as to how they would plan the attack against their individual target. There were no large, Pathfinder-type operations, it was one bomber and one target. One way of increasing experience on the type and the ability to operate over long distances alone was to send aircraft on 'Lone Rangers' across the globe. Initially RAF stations across the UK were visited, then Luqa, Malta became a regular Mediterranean hop. Air Vice-Marshal Kenneth 'Bing' Cross, the Air Officer Commanding of 3 Group (later C-in-C Bomber Command), of which 10 Squadron was part, participated in the first real long-distance Lone Ranger as part of the crew of XA938 which travelled from Gaydon, via Goose Bay and Offutt AFB to California on October 13, 1958. Cross was in California to watch the annual SAC Bombing Competition, which RAF bombers would take part in to not only compete, but to evaluate procedures and ideas with their American counterparts. Both the USA and Canada would prove to be the real training grounds for the Victors, the UK, being so small offered few challenges from a navigation point of view, especially for an experienced crew.

By this time, a second Victor B.1 unit, 15 Squadron was reformed at Cottesmore on September 1, 1958.

DISPERSAL

The V-force was put on the back foot very early on when the Soviets began to deploy nuclear-tipped medium range missiles in all their satellite territories from 1958. Such weapons would devastate the V-force within minutes, a single weapon would easily neutralise an RAF station like Cottesmore. In response, the government's Defence White Paper of 1958 announced, firstly, that efforts were in hand to increase the V-force's state of readiness so that the amount of time from scramble to take off could be minimised. A second, slightly more cryptic message in the white paper stated that action was being taken 'to increase the security of the bomber force'. The other action was quite simply to disperse the aircraft to pre-chosen secondary airfields in times of real tension.

The Victor's potential target range took it as far east as Magnitogorsk on the Ural River. Targets included the Volga oilfields and all the Ukrainian iron and steel plants as well as 72 USSR cities which had a population of 200,000 or more. Great faith was put in the Victor force, although Gp Capt Johnson confessed that the Victors would have been highly vulnerable in daylight if we dared to take part in a war not including the USA. However, with US support and combined with their own nuclear strikes, up to 90% of the V-force was predicted to have reached their targets if the main strike was at night. With the arrival of RAF Fylingdales in 1962, Early Warning Radar was now part of the package, and it became the 'norm' to place one Victor on Quick Reaction Alert (QRA) at the home base in the event of a surprise attack.

VICTOR NUKES

Both 10 and 15 Squadrons spent most of 1958 and early 1959 working up to an operational standard with conventional weapons. 10 Squadron recorded that it was not until November 1959 that a practise scramble was conducted with 10,000lb drill and inert weapons. Regular nuclear weapons courses were being attended at Bomber Command Bombing School, Lindholme, and by early 1960 specialist armament teams, from newly formed Armament Supports Flight were employed specifically to load and unload all nuclear-type weapons. **≫**

The original plan was to deploy Britain's first atomic bomb, codenamed *Blue Danube*, to the Victor squadrons, the 10-12 kiloton weapons, having been stockpiled at nearby Wittering since 1953. A Vickers Valiant flight was meant to introduce the *Blue Danube* into service but instead the weapon was retired by 1962 without being deployed. One weapon that would see service was *Yellow Sun* Mk.1, with a '*Green Grass*' 400 kiloton plutonium and hydrogen warhead. Weighing in a 7,250lb and measuring 21ft long, *Yellow Sun* did not take up a great deal of room in the bomb bay of a Victor. Introduced into service from 1959, *Yellow Sun* Mk.II followed in 1961. The warhead (A US W-28) for this weapon was called '*Red Snow*' and yielded a colossal 1.1 Megatons. *Yellow Sun* Mk.II would serve as Britain's primary air-dropped strategic nuclear weapon until the arrival of WE.177B in 1966. The latter would serve briefly with the Victor B.2 force but was destined to remain in service into the late 1990s.

The US owned and controlled Mark 5 nuclear bomb was also available to the Victor, 72 of which were available to the V-force until withdrawn in 1963. Another weapon which entered service in 1962 was *Red Beard*, Britain's first tactical nuclear weapon.

Produced in two versions, the Mk.1 was designed for high-altitude delivery and Mk.2, low-level. *Red Beard* was also superseded by WE.177B and was finally withdrawn in 1971.

The Avro-manufactured *Blue Steel* nuclear standoff missile entered service in 1963 and was destined to only equip the Victor B.2. The 35ft 1in-long missile weighed in at 17,000lb and with a *Red Snow* warhead, had a 1.1 Megaton power. The weapon was recessed into the bomb bay of the Victor, and when carried, one of the four tail fins of the weapon had to be folded in the horizontal to allow for ground clearance. Being an Avro weapon, *Blue Steel* was designed specifically with the Vulcan in mind, an aircraft with a considerably higher ground clearance than the Victor, which only offered a ground clearance below the weapon of 14in. However, this had no effect on the rotation of the aircraft and the weapon was destined to serve with both the Victor and Vulcan until the country's nuclear deterrent responsibility was handed to the Royal Navy.

CONVENTIONAL POTENTIAL

Although the primary role of the Victor force was the delivery of a nuclear weapon or in other words, a nuclear deterrent, the Victor's secondary role, as in 1954, was to 'supplement tactical bomber forces if the need arises by delivering maximum weight of High Explosive bombs by night, and if practicable by day, on targets at relatively short distance from base'. The Victor's conventional capability was incredible, the aircraft's bomb bay was 34ft long, 9ft wide and 7ft deep giving it the potential to carry an eye-watering 48 1,000lb bombs! Handley Page had also devised underwing bomb carriers which had the

potential to give the aircraft a bombload of 76 1,000lb bombs, although the range of bomber would have suffered dramatically. Operationally, the RAF capped the maximum bombload at a 'mere' 35 1,000lb bombs. There were some delays in the production of the conventional bombing equipment and trials did not begin until June 1959 when XA921 successfully dropped 35 1,000lb bombs. As a result, the aircraft was cleared for conventional bombing from 14,000ft and higher, although for long-range operations, the load would be reduced to 21,000lb which would make room for an extra fuel tank in the front of the bomb bay.

Two more Victor units were reformed at RAF Honington, both destined to be associated with the type the longest by some margin, beginning with 57 Squadron on January 1, 1959, followed by 55 Squadron on September 1, 1960. Both 10 and 15 Squadron's service with the Victor B.1 and B.1A was short; 10 Squadron disbanded on March 1, 1964, while 15 squadron disbanded on October 1, 1964. These two squadron's commitments in the Far East (specifically the Malayan Emergency) were taken over by 55 and 57 Squadron. The very presence of the Victors operating from Butterworth and Tengah can be credited with helping, slowly, to diffuse the situation which peaked in late 1964.

LOW-LEVEL WEAPON DELIVERY

The art of high-level bombing, over Europe at least, was already considered a very dangerous occupation thanks to the shooting down of the Lockheed U-2 spy plane flown by Gary Powers on May 1, 1960. Brought down from 70,000ft by a Soviet SAM, the Victor's maximum ceiling was much less. Having already shelved the *Blue Steel* Mk.2 medium range ballistic missile all eyes turned to the US Douglas GAM-87 *Skybolt* air-launched ballistic missile which had a range of 300 miles. In early 1960, an order for 144 *Skybolts* was placed, and trials began in the US, using B-52s and a Vulcan. Unfortunately, *Skybolt* was cancelled in 1963. The more powerful and longer-range *Blue Steel* Mk.2 was studied (cancelled in 1960 in favour of *Skybolt*) and Handley Page briefly conducted some Victor compatibility work, but it was too little, too late as by the time the missile would be ready, *Polaris* would have been in service.

The cancellation of *Skybolt* had left the V-force in an awkward position, the Victor B.1 for example would have been fitted with an advanced enemy communications jammer but this was cancelled because the range of *Skybolt* meant that the aircraft would not have needed to penetrate enemy defences. Some improvements were introduced including the *Red Steer* tail warning radar, which was installed in the rear fuselage, within a blunt tail cone. This new electronic countermeasure (ECM) required powerful transmitters which were cooled with a glycol system. Crew positions were also revised for the new equipment and this new variant, designated as the Victor B.1A first entered service with 57 Squadron.

BELOW: Victor B.2 XL158 of No.139 Squadron with a *Blue Steel* stand-off nuclear bomb recessed into its bomb bay. (Andrew Hay – flyingart.co.uk)

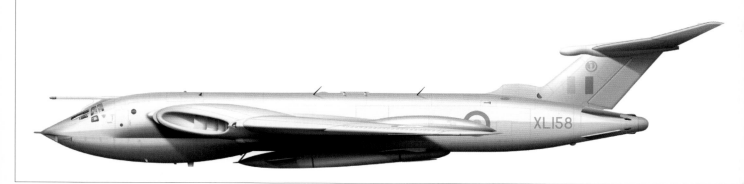

ABOVE:
Two Handley-Page Victors each carrying a *Blue Steel* stand-off missile recessed into their bomb bays. Also visible in this view are their underwing fuel tanks, protruding forward of the wing and their 'Küchemann carrots' jutting behind each wing. The latter were aerodynamic efficiency aids introduced with the B.2 variant.
(KEY Archive)

From early 1963 the Aeroplane & Armament Experimental Establishment (A&AEE) began several trials to assess how well the Victor would perform during prolonged low-level flight and to develop new methods of delivering the weapon to the target. It was quickly discovered the Victor performed exceptionally well at low-level and the A&AEE quickly gave clearance to squadrons to begin training for low-level operations at speeds up to 350kts. Using southwest England as the initial training ground, A&AEE pilots described how easy it was to terrain follow in the aircraft, with the throttles fixed in a set position. The aircraft's speed would only vary by 20kts as it gently climbed and descended. For the Victor B.1 crews at Cottesmore and Honington, no low-level nuclear weapon would arrive and as a result the A&AEE worked on methods of delivering high-level bombs from low level. It was a simple solution, where the aircraft would 'pop-up' from a fixed pull-up point, then conduct a constant attitude climb to 9,000ft before releasing the bomb load and making a quick escape turn and descending to low level again. Low-level operations down to 250ft made no additional demands on the Victor B.1/1As navigation and bombing equipment. Range trials revealed that this method of attack improved accuracy to within 250yds of the centre of the target. Flying so low, the pilots could also map read, passing fixes back to the navigation team.

THE VICTOR B.2 – ADVANTAGE REGAINED

The Rolls-Royce Conway-powered Victor B.2 first entered RAF service with 139 Squadron at Wittering in February 1962. The second, and final unit to receive the Victor B.2 was 100 Squadron, also based at Wittering. Equipped with the *Blue Steel* missile, the original tactics for these two units, collectively known as the Wittering Wing, was to attack a single target at high-level. But, as already mentioned, the new method was now low-level which effectively reduced the range of the *Blue Steel* from 200

miles to 25 to 30 miles. It was not all doom and gloom as the Soviet strategy with its fighter and missile defence was designed with a high level in mind and could not cope with a multi-pronged, single aircraft attack at low altitude. En route, the Victor would approach the Soviet defences at altitude to conserve fuel and then on approaching the defence network, would descend to below 1,000ft. Undetectable to radar below this height, the Victor could have easily breached the Soviets vast, and incredibly extensive network of radar and missile systems. At that time Soviet fighter aircrafts' airborne radar did not have the capable to look down below 5,000ft, the pilot only having his eyes to pick out a single bomber aircraft, potentially attacking at night in poor weather conditions. To add to the defender's woes, the traditional all white, anti-flash scheme worn by all V-force aircraft was substituted for camouflaged upper surfaces which were incredibly effective when flying at low-level. This scheme was first introduced on a 139 Squadron Victor in December 1963.

The Victor B.2 was quickly cleared for low-level operations, the aircraft, with its large 'Küchemann carrots' (aerodynamic fairings) on each wing, which had proved to delay the formation of shock waves at high speed, made the aircraft particularly suited to ground-hugging sorties. Tactics were simple, on approaching the target, sufficient height was gained to allow the *Blue Steel* to fall away and fire its twin chamber Armstrong Siddeley Stentor Mk.101 rocket engine. Climbing to 17,000ft at Mach 1.5, the engine would then cut out and in theory hit the target with an accuracy of 300yds.

From 1963 onwards, the *Blue Steel* equipped Wittering Wing would continue the Victor element of the V-force until disbandment came for both units in late 1968 – 100 Squadron on September 30, and 139 Squadron on December 31.

The most dangerous period of the Cold War may have been ending for the RAF, but the Cold War and a literally 'MAD' (mutually assured destruction) period of this planet's history would rumble on into the early 1990s.

Victor Tanker Force

Chris Pierce presents a brief history of the Handley Page Victor in its near 30-year 'second' career in the air-to-air refuelling role.

MAIN PICTURE:
Handley Page selected a single aircraft, Victor B.1, XA918, for conversion to a tanker. It undertook trials with the A&AEE at Boscombe Down from 1963-1968.
(KEY Archive)

A Valiant replacement was needed – and it was needed fast! The narrator of a Pathé news film from 1957 *The Last Valiant* had said: "she'll be in first-line service for years to come." They could not, unfortunately, have been further from the truth. It was from July 1964, that the rapid decline of the Valiant began when serious cracks were found in the rear spars of several aircraft. The near catastrophic failure of a 232 OCU Valiant operating out of RAF Gaydon on August 6, 1964, sealed the type's fate. This was despite a potential, if costly, rectification programme quickly beginning, which would have meant the type remaining in service considerably longer, just like its stable mates. The one crucial role that the Valiant, and specifically 90 and 214 Squadrons, would need replacing swiftly, was air-to-air refuelling. These two squadrons alone had dramatically extended the capability of both RAF Fighter and Bomber Command, with proving flights from the UK and Singapore direct and even an epic operation in 1961 when a single Vulcan was supported from the UK non-stop to Australia.

WELL-TIMED SOLUTION

Despite having only entered service in April 1958, by 1964 the Handley Page Victor B.1 was being withdrawn from RAF service in favour of the B.2 variant. Two of the four squadrons which were equipped with the Victor B.1, namely 10 and 15 Squadrons, were disbanded in March and October 1964 respectively, their aircraft becoming surplus to requirements.

Prior to this, Handley Page had selected a single aircraft, Victor B.1, XA918, for conversion to a tanker. This aircraft was initially being converted with wing-mounted Flight Refuelling FR.20B hose-drogue pods under each outer wing. The original plan was to make these pods interchangeable with under-wing tanks or 'Red Necks' (Side-Looking Airborne Radar housed in a long underwing pods) mounted to the standard strong points. However, that would position the trailing drogues too close to the tail unit, so the idea was scrubbed. XA918 was delivered to the Aeroplane & Armament Experiment Establishment (A&AEE) at Boscombe Down for evaluation as a tanker, the first of many trials at the Wiltshire airfield beginning on August 3, 1963.

XA918 was destined to visit Boscombe no less than eight times, the final trial not ending until August 10, 1967.

It was not until the impending demise of the Valiant tanker force and the combination of a number of Victor B.1 and B.1A airframes delivered to Radlett from 10 and 15 Squadron's disbandment, that Handley Page was in a good position to quickly fill the RAF's air-to-air refuelling capability. The company was already working flat out converting nine Victor SR.2s for 543 Squadron and had also begun a 24-hour shift pattern at its Colney Street site to convert six Victor B.1As into two-point tankers, the same configuration as XA918.

XA918 would also be converted in the more useful three-point configuration which, as well as the FR.20 pods under each wing, also had a FR.17 hose-drogue pack installed the bomb bay. Ten Victor B.1s and 14 B.1As would be converted to three-point standard and be designated as K.1s, while the first six aircraft, which still retained their bombing capability were designated as B(K).1As. XH620 was the first B(K).1A to take to air on April 28, 1965 and all six of this variant were delivered to 55 Squadron, which had moved from RAF

Honington to Marham on May 24, 1965, the unit soon becoming operational on the type. It is worth noting at this point that the last air-to-air refuelling sortie by a Valiant was by XD812 of 214 Squadron on December 9, 1964.

Operational trials were performed with the English Electric Lightnings of 19 Squadron flying from RAF Leconfield in August. The Lightning was a notoriously thirsty fighter that relied heavily on air-to-air refuelling to perform air defence duties right up until its withdrawal in the late 1980s.

The first three-point K.1 tanker was XA937, the aircraft conducting its maiden flight on November 3, 1965. This variant was issued to 57 Squadron, also at RAF Marham, in February 1966, the unit becoming operational on June 1, 1966. Early operational trials for 57 Squadron included the first air-to-air refuel of a 10 Squadron Vickers VC10 in October 1966.

A new Tanker Training Flight (TTF) was also formed at Marham on July 1, 1965, from the Victor tanker element of 232 OCU at Gaydon, which had been disbanded the day before. The unit operated the Victor B.1, B.1A and K.1A as well as a Chipmunk in support. The TTF was disbanded into the Victor Training Unit on October 13, 1969, a ➤➤

ABOVE: The original idea to have interchangeable refuelling pods that could be swapped for alternative types of operational equipment was dropped on safety grounds. (KEY Archive)

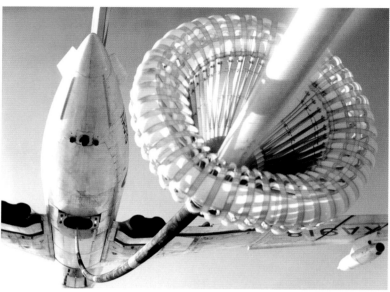

short-lived outfit that was absorbed into the reformed 232 OCU on February 6, 1970, which continued to provide training on the type until June 30, 1986.

Synonymous with pioneering Valiant air-to-air techniques, 214 Squadron was reformed at Marham on July 1, 1966, equipped with Victor K.1. While 55 Squadron was re-equipped with the Victor K.1 and K.1A, its part-bombing capability now removed for good.

THE VICTOR K.2

The contract to convert the next wave of tankers from the Victor B.2 and SR.2 fleet was technically agreed in October 1969. The initial design and feasibility studies were conducted by Handley Page staff, while the actual build contract was awarded to Hawker Siddeley Aviation (HAS) Ltd. at Woodford. The entire programme was fully transferred by August 1970, by which time the receivers had done their worst and Handley Page was no more. HSA would now handle the support of the in-service Victor K.1s and K.1As, all operating from Marham with 55, 57 and 214 Squadrons and 232 OCU and the SR.2s of 543 Squadron, operating out of Wyton.

An order for 29 Victor K.2 conversions, using B.2 and SR.2 airframes was placed by the RAF but by the spring of 1975 Treasury cuts had reduced this to 24 aircraft. The prototype Victor K.2 was XL231 which first flew from Woodford on March 1, 1972. The K.2 had its wingspan reduced from the original 120ft down to 113ft to extend the fatigue life of the reconditioned airframes. Following successful trials of the prototype with the A&AEE, the Victor K.2 entered RAF service on May 8, 1974, with 232 OCU at Marham. 55 Squadron first received the K.2 in July 1975, 57 Squadron in June 1976 while 214 Squadron was destined to keep its K.1s until it was disbanded on January 28, 1977.

The Victor K.2 served with great distinction during the Falklands War (see page 54), and it is difficult to comprehend the air campaign being conducted so efficiently without the RAF's elite group of tanker aircraft. Flying out of Wideawake airfield, located on the solitary mid-Atlantic island of Ascension, the Victors racked up more than 3,000hrs of flying time between April and June 1982. Approximately 600 air-to-air refuelling sorties were performed in support of the Nimrod, Vulcan, Harrier, and the slower-flying C-130 Hercules, the latter involving a very challenging technique.

By the late 1980s the end was in sight for the venerable aircraft, beginning with the disbandment of 57 Squadron and 232 OCU on June 30, 1986. This left 55 Squadron as the sole Victor unit with approximately 15 aircraft on

strength. There would be one more chance for the Victor to shine before retirement, and this came with the Gulf War of 1991. 55 Squadron deployed eight Victor K.2s to the Gulf as part of *Operation Granby*, (see page 54) the main customers being the Sepecat Jaguar and Panavia Tornado, the first sortie being conducted on January 18, 1991. By the end of the conflict, 55 Squadron had flown 299 sorties before returning to Marham for the final time. The axe finally fell on October 15, 1993, with the disbandment of 55 Squadron, many of the unit's aircraft being 'deployed' to museums around the country.

ACCIDENTS AND INCIDENTS

The accident rate of the RAF's Victor tanker force, considering the very high number of sorties/flying hours accumulated over 30 years, was incredibly low. However, a total of eight aircrew lost their lives in five major accidents, the first occurring on August 19, 1968.

At approximately 2200hrs, the pilot, Sqn Ldr M T Doyle, of TTF Victor K.1A, XH646, reported: "I am at 13,500ft and climbing….". It was at that very moment that the Victor collided with a 213 Squadron Canberra B(I).6 returning from a practise bombing on a local range having set course for home to Brüggen in Germany. All four crew aboard the Victor and three in the Canberra stood no chance as both aircraft broke up and scattered themselves across Kelling Heath, northeast of Holt in North Norfolk. The accident was blamed on a combination of very poor weather conditions and a lack of coverage of surveillance radar, it later being noted that both aircraft were in a blind spot when the collision took place.

The next incident was destined to be the only occasion that a Victor was lost during air-to-air refuelling duties and in this case, only dry run hook-ups were being practised for the benefit of the receiver aircraft, whose pilot was building experience on type. The incident took place over the North Sea 100 miles east of Sunderland. The tanker, 57 Squadron, Victor K.1A, XH618 was being flown by Flt Lt K Handscomb, while the receiver aircraft was 237 OCU, Buccaneer S.2A, XV156, one of three such aircraft flying from RAF Honington. The plan was for the pilot of XV156 to conduct a few dry connections to the drogue which was initially conducted successfully on the starboard side hose. The pilot of XV156 then repositioned the aircraft to connect to the port side hose, but this time approached too fast. To avoid striking the Victor the Buccaneer pilot pulled up quickly but the aircraft's probe still struck the port drogue basket forcing the machine to ascend between the port wing and tailplane. Unfortunately, the Buccaneer then stalled and dropped on the port side of the Victor's tailplane, slicing the surface completely away. The Victor instantly bunted over, pinning all of the crew into their seats under extreme negative 'G' forces. However, Flt Lt Handscomb somehow managed to eject before the Victor exploded killing the four remaining crew instantly. It has been suggested that Handscomb may have been 'ejected' from the aircraft as the aircraft broke up. More testament to the construction of the Buccaneer, XV156 flew home to Honington with little damage.

55 Squadron suffered its first Victor tanker loss on September 29, 1975. Victor K.2, XL513 had already begun to rotate during the take-off run when at least one seagull entered an engine at a speed of approximately 166mph. The captain of the aircraft took the quick decision to abandon the take-off, most likely knowing full well that there would not be enough runway left to stop the aircraft safely. As a result, and despite deploying the large brake parachute and applying very heavy braking, the Victor careered into the overshoot area, ripping off one main undercarriage unit and seriously damaged the fuselage structure to such a degree the aircraft was a write-off but, more importantly, the crew were safe.

The next incident also involved a 55 Squadron on the runway but on this occasion the aircraft had only moved a few feet before it was brought to a swift halt. It was October 15, 1982 and Victor K.2, XL232 had taxied to the end of Marham's main runway without incident. Moments after the throttles had been pushed forward, one of the Rolls-Royce Conway engines suffered a turbine failure. All

engines were shut down immediately and the aircraft was quickly evacuated by all five crew where it stood. Despite the fire service responding quickly, the aircraft was engulfed by fire and was destroyed rapidly by its own huge fuel load.

The final accident in RAF service came on June 19, 1986 and involved 55 Squadron, Victor K.2, XL191. The aircraft was attempting an Instrument Landing System (ILS) approach to Hamilton Airport, Ontario but failed to pick up the signal, resulting in the crew taking on a visual approach through cloud. Unfortunately, the runway was misidentified and when the error was realised the pilot attempted to realign with the correct runway at very low level and with little room for manoeuvre. Whilst within half a mile of the runway the aircraft pitched down slightly and struck the ground 300ft short before bouncing back in the air again. The Victor then ground looped and came to rest 1,500ft from the original impact point; luckily all five crewmembers escaped unharmed, but XL191 was a complete write off. A subsequent investigation determined poor crew co-operation was the main cause of the accident.

Following the Victor's retirement from the RAF in 1993, several airframes were scattered around the country for preservation, two of them, were kept in taxiable condition: XL231 *Lusty Lindy* at Elvington and XM715 *Teasin' Tina/ Victor Meldrew* at Bruntingthorpe. It was the latter that was involved in the type's final 'incident', when on May 3, 2009, XM715 accidentally took off during what was intended to be a high-speed taxi run. With experienced Victor pilot Bob Prothero at the controls the aircraft was quickly brought back under control, becoming the last of its type to take to the air, albeit for a very short distance!

BELOW: **Handley Page Victor K.2 XL164 of 57 Squadron refuels XL191 of 55 Squadron. The latter aircraft was written-off in a 1986 landing accident, but its crew survived the ordeal.** (KEY Archive)

A final top-up with 57 Squadron

Malcolm English was privileged to join 57 Squadron for an air-to-air refuelling sortie just before the unit retired its long-serving Handley Page Victor K.2s.

When 57 squadron disbanded on June 30, 1986, it was almost 60 years to the day since its formation. At that time, due to a quirk of fate, it had been operational for 57 years. The squadron had flown a previous generation of Britain's nuclear deterrent, the Boeing Washington B.1 from 1951 and, two years later, in May 1953 it received its first jets – English Electric Canberra B.2s – which it flew until disbandment on December 9, 1957.

It reformed on January 1, 1959, at Honington as part of the Medium Bomber Force flying Victor B.1s. On June 1, 1966, it moved to Marham in Norfolk, where it became an in-flight refuelling squadron with Victor K.1s. It received its first Victor K.2s in 1976.

VICTORS AT MARHAM

At the time of my visit to Marham in March 1986, there were 22 Victors on the strength of 232 Operational Conversion Unit (OCU) and the two resident squadrons numbers 55 and 57. Both squadrons were established for eight aircraft and the OCU for three, the remaining three machines were held in reserve. With the disbandment of 232 OCU on April 4 and 57 Squadron that June, 55 Squadron was expected to comprise 15 aircraft including five in reserve. Some airframes were retained as spares depending on their remaining fatigue life. Perhaps surprisingly, considering the run-down of the Victor fleet, there was still a need for an OCU and to that end, 55 Squadron became a 13-crew unit, the extra three crews essentially forming a training flight while remaining still very much part of the squadron. Three crews were still being trained per year.

Being a valuable resource in great demand by all the United Kingdom and RAF Germany air assets, including the Royal Navy, the tanker force was controlled by No.1 Group Strike Command. Units submitted monthly bids and No.1 Group appropriated either flying hours or a fuel allowance. The Tanker Planning Cell within operations then liaised with receiver units on a daily or weekly basis.

Typical of the tasks allocated 257 Squadron was that on March 12, 1986, in which refuelling support was requested by the Royal Navy for Sea Harriers embarked in HMS *Ark Royal*. To maximise the training opportunity for the tanker crews and also to demonstrate the Victor's buddy-buddy refuelling technique, the squadron allocated two aircraft for the exercise, Victor K.2s XM717 and XL160. The latter was on temporary detachment to Finningley, Yorkshire, where its crew were instructing.

Crews for the sortie were: XM717 - Wg Cdr David Hayward, captain; Flt Lt Steve Mclaughlin, co-pilot; F/O Nick Barber, nav radar; Flt Lt Dave Taylor, nav plotter; Flt Lt Pete Langan, air electronics officer (AEO); and me in the sixth seat; XL160 – Flt Lt Gary Weightman, captain; F/O Stuart Mitchell, co-pilot; F/O Brain Boyle, nav radar; Flt Lt Angus Deas, nav plotter; and F/O Martin Andrews AEO.

Having been inspected and passed as fit by the base doctor, I was kitted out in the safety equipment section. Unfortunately, as we would be operating near the coast, I was obliged to wear a 'goon suit' - that most uncomfortable rubber immersion suit. My next visit was to Victor B.1, XA917, – or to be more precise – its nose section, which is used for crew drill training. XA917's claim to fame is that in addition to being the first production Victor, it also 'inadvertently' exceeded the speed of sound on June 1, 1957, in a shallow dive at 40,000ft. The speed, according to a plaque on the side of the crew trainer was Mach 1.1015; goodness knows how it was derived so accurately. Nevertheless, it is testament to the Victor's excellent transonic handling characteristics that there were no noticeable trim changes or buffet.

The sixth seat is probably the easiest of them all to egress from in the event of an emergency on the ground as it is immediately next to the cockpit door. However, when I made to follow Pete Langan out of the door during a practise emergency evacuation, it seemed to take an eternity while I fumbled to release Martin-Baker catches, oxygen hoses and seat belt lock. As the second to exit, I was sure that in the event of a genuine emergency there would be a real risk of receiving four pairs of boot prints on my back – either to 'assist' me out, or as the crew called 'goodbye'! >>

An escape in flight would be infinitely easier. Once the door is open, a sharp pull on a button on the side of the seat and an inflatable cushion forces the occupant out of the seat and through the door. The crew stations are almost identical to those in the Vulcan, and, like its delta-winged counterpart, the Victor only had ejection seats for the pilot and co-pilot. A scheme to incorporate a jettisonable capsule was abandoned early in the design stage, although provision was made in the prototype for the separation of the pressure cabin by explosive bolts.

Briefing consisted of the usual weather, NOTAM, weight/speeds, navigation, radio, and task details. Weather was the only concern with fog reducing visibility to around 500ft. Although this would not prevent us taking off, if it worsened, we would have to divert. Valley and Brize Norton were the primary and secondary diversion airfields, respectively. Our task was to refuel four Sea Harriers of 801 Squadron, as required, which were flying from HMS *Ark Royal*. We were to 'dry-pod' from XL160, after which the roles would reverse, and Garry Weightman would practise dry-podding with us. The refuelling area for the exercise was 'Towline 7', a racetrack pattern bounded at each end by Yeovilton, Somerset, and St Mawgan, Cornwall.

Due to the changes in the requested rendezvous, the pre-flight lunch was rather hurried (albeit most welcome), after which we boarded the crew bus for the trip out to the flight line. The met forecast was wrong. Instead of the visibility improving around midday as predicted it was, if anything, worse and it looked as if I would be sampling Valley or Brize Norton's hospitality. Our hemp-coloured Victor appeared most wraith-like in the mist; even the port refuelling pod was camouflaged adding to the effect. While David Hayward signed the necessary forms, the rest of the crew boarded the aircraft, strapped in, and began preparing for flight. I and my camera were last.

CRAMPED COCKPIT

Considering the immense size of the Victor – it is 114ft 11in-long – the cockpit is extremely cramped. The sixth seat is immediately behind the pilot's and co-pilot's seats and in addition to swivelling to ease egress, can slide forwards to the edge of the front seat well. The two navigators and AEO faced rearwards with the nav radar on the starboard side, nav plotter in the centre and AEO on the port side.

The nav radar was primarily responsible for the monitoring, controlling, and planning the refuelling operation. He was the acknowledged expert, having a detailed knowledge of the receivers' needs – Including quirks such as the Lightning's preference for warm fuel – speeds and heights, and gave a running commentary of the situation as seen through his periscope. Benefiting his title, he was also able to assist the nav plotter in such tasks as taking astro shots. The Victor's H2S radar set, although utilising old technology, was still a useful piece of equipment and in addition to its normal function had been used for weather avoidance and even to assist in positioning for landing.

Traditional navigation was performed by the nav plotter for which he was provided with a range of equipment including Omega, Tacan, and Doppler. Omega was fitted for the Victor's Falklands tasks and was considered by the crews to be one of the most useful pieces of equipment in the aircraft. Communications and the aircraft's electrical system were the responsibility of the AEO. The brief task description belied his high workload. Of the two front crew members, the captain was responsible primarily for flying the aircraft and was in overall command while the co-pilot managed the fuel control system and assisted the captain to fly the aircraft.

A brief message from the control tower informed us that Victor XL160 was airborne so, having checked that all systems were functioning correctly and obtaining take-off clearance, we taxied to runway 06. Lined-up at the end of the runway with the lights disappearing into the murk, David Haywood completed the pre take-off checks, advanced the throttles and released the brakes.

At an all-up weight of 193,000lb our rotation speed was 140kts. Even with the four 20,600lb-thrust Rolls-Royce Conway Mk.201 turbofans at 80%, our climb rate at 240kts was a respectable 4,000ft per minute or so

BELOW: **Victor K.2 XL160 displays its unique and graceful lines – photographed through the radar navigator's window of Victor K.2 XM717 in March 1986.** (Malcolm English)

ABOVE: **Flying Officer Nick Barber with periscope in hand. Note that the H2S radar screen is blank as it became unserviceable shortly after take-off during the March 1986 sortie in which Victor K.2 XM717 of 57 Squadron refuelled Sea Harriers embarked on HMS *Ark Royal*.** (Malcolm English)

RIGHT: **The crew of 57 Squadron Victor K.2 XM717 for the sortie in March 1986 during which it refuelled three Sea Harriers embarked on HMS *Ark Royal*. Wg Cdr David Hayward, captain; Flt Lt Steve McLaughlin, co-pilot; F/O Nick Barber, nav radar; Flt Lt Dave Taylor, nav plotter; Flt Lt Pete Langan, AEO. (NB crew not necessarily photographed in order listed above).** (Malcolm English)

and the flaps and undercarriage were smartly retracted to avoid exceeding their limiting speeds of 225 and 235kts, respectively. During the climb we turned right onto a heading of 235°, levelled at our cruise height of flight level (FL) 270 (27,000ft) and accelerated to 300kts.

The previous week I had driven to Yeovilton from my village in Bedfordshire and been pleased at the relatively short time of the journey, some two hours; in XM717 I arrived overhead Yeovilton less than 35 minutes after take-off having travelled at least 50 miles more than on my car trip. XL160 was visually seen at a distance of around ten miles having been vectored onto it by ground control and using our air-to- air Tacan. The three Sea Harriers in formation (one did not appear) with the Victor had refuelled by the time we arrived at the 'Towline' and two departed immediately after our sighting, to continue their exercise.

Maintaining a 2,000ft height separation with the Victor / Sea Harrier formation we offered fuel to 'Silver 3' – the Sea Harriers' call sign – which he accepted. There are many procedures a receiver can adopt to join a tanker. These range from a silent join up – the method which would be used in wartime – to those using radio and perhaps ground control radar. Silver 3 positioned on our port side, too far aft, unfortunately, for me to take a photograph and having received clearance slid back to position immediately behind our port hose which had been trailed by Nick Barber.

Observing the Sea Harrier through the periscope as it closed, Nick called out its position. There was no apparent response in the Victor as Silver 3 contacted the hose although there could, apparently, be quite a trim change within the larger receivers. Four minutes later, having received 4,000lb of fuel, the Sea Harrier disengaged and held station while I attempted to take photographs through the periscope. The periscope had an included angular scan of 60° which is more than sufficient an arc in which receivers would lie when refuelling from the wing pods.

DRY POD

No sooner had Silver 3 departed, *Ark Royal* called to thank us for 'looking after her chicks'. Still orbiting in the 'Towline 7' pattern, Victor XL160 was now ahead and 1,000ft above us at 27,000 feet. Basically, repeating the procedure adopted by the Sea Harrier, David Haywood accelerated gently and climbed to bring us up to FL270, astern of XL160 for a practise dry pod. There we stabilised about 10ft from the centreline or Hose Drum Unit (HDU) refuelling drogue.

Visual references on the underside of the tanker were used for accurate positioning rather than try to 'fly' the probe into the drogue.

David then inched the throttle forward to achieve a closing speed of three to 5kts and with deceptive ease, engaged the drogue. In the few seconds prior to the engagement, it was somewhat disconcerting to see the large "shuttlecock" apparently hovering only a couple of feet above the canopy. Once engaged, the basket was forced forwards 7ft or so, thus triggering a microswitch in the HDU which allowed fuel to flow.

Although ours was a dry pod, such is the Victor's HDU plumbing circuitry that unless the receiver closes his tanks, fuel would flow under gravity with a flow rate of about 1,000lb per minute. With the fuel pump on, this is increased to some 5,000lb per minute, depending upon the receiver. That phenomenon did not occur with the pods. Disengaging from XL160 there was slight turbulence as we passed through the tanker's wake. Another dry pod, as smooth as the first, just to show his co-pilot how it should be done, then we disengaged and XL160 dropped below us to reverse the roles. With our speed still at 270kts Gary Weightman made six smooth contacts, receiving 4,000lb of fuel in the process.

At 1340hrs, having been on task for 45 minutes, we set course for Marham. XL160 formed up in loose formation on our starboard side for photographs prior to letting down into the murk for landing. Fortunately, the weather had not deteriorated and with a declared minimum decision height of 200ft, we broke through the overcast at 300ft and 150kts. With the runway lights dead ahead, Steve McLaughlin performed a touch-and-go and this was followed by a full-stop landing by David Hayward at 1440hrs. No sooner had the nose wheel touched the runway than our brake parachute was streamed and nosewheel steering engaged. Nosewheel steering is achieved using a wheel on the pilot's side of the cockpit. Therefore, if the pilot lands the aircraft the co-pilot must take over control of the column.

Our first stop after disembarking was to the engineering section for a debrief. Two snags were reported - the complete failure of our radar immediately after take-off and a malfunctioning Identification Friend or Foe (IFF) set.

Back then to the flight planning room to complete the necessary paperwork; a quick crew debrief – everything had gone according to plan – shed the hated goon suit and it was time to relax in 57 Squadron's crew room.

The Victor soldiered on with the RAF until 1993, slightly longer than was expected at the time of my flight and proved to be a capable platform throughout its service life.

Warzones!

Thankfully, the Victor was never used in the role it was originally designed for, but it played an important supporting role in the Falklands conflict (1982) and Gulf War One (1991). **Chris Pierce** reports.

On April 2, 1982, Argentina invaded the Falkland Islands followed, the next day, by South Georgia. The British government was very quick to respond and on April 5 a large naval task force, comprising 127 ships, set sail to recover the islands.

The vast distances involved would mean that there was no doubt that the RAF's small but efficient Victor tanker force, would play a major role in what was to be known as *Operation Corporate*. By now, there were only 24 Victor K.2s on strength between 55 and 57 Squadrons based at Marham and it would literally be every man to the pumps if their contribution was to be a success.

On April 18, both squadrons were ready to detach six Victors between them to Wideawake airfield on Ascension Island in the mid-Atlantic. It was a large, well-equipped airfield which still lay approximately 2,850 miles away from South Georgia. This small island, 850 miles east of the Falklands would be the first objective for the British forces. The first priority was reconnaissance, and the task force needed plenty of it before any ground or sea operations in the area could begin. The untimely disbandment of 27 Squadron and its Vulcan B.2(MRR) aircraft on March 31 did not help the situation, so the Victor temporarily also served as a reconnaissance aircraft. All the Victor force was quickly updated with the latest »

MAIN PICTURE:
All the Handley Page Victors operating during *Operation Granby* **were painted in the desert hemp colour scheme.** (Mick Dodsworth)

"We are going to war tonight; it starts at midnight".

ABOVE:

A veteran of
*Operation
Corporate*
(Falklands) and
Granby (Gulf
War One) XH672,
'Maid Marian', is
on public display
at the RAF
Museum Cosford.
(KEY Archive)

navigation equipment and a camera fitted in the nose of each aircraft. The first tasking was to support one of their own on a reconnaissance sortie.

At 0250hrs on April 20, Victor K.2, XL192 took off from Wideawake, captained by Squadron Leader J Elliott, a man familiar with aerial reconnaissance from his days with 543 Squadron. In support of this Victor sortie to South Georgia were four other Victor K.2s, each of them taking off within a minute of each other from Wideawake. Approximately 1,000 miles south of Ascension, two of the Victors transferred all their spare fuel to the other two aircraft, who continued towards South Georgia, while the other pair returned to Ascension. After another 1,000 miles was flown, a final refuelling was carried out between the three aircraft, and it was at this point that Elliot and his crew were on their own.

Dawn had broken when South Georgia was in sight, the Victor descending from its cruising height of 43,000ft to 18,000ft so that the navigator radar could use his H2S to scan the area for 'blips'. Within 90 minutes, 150,000 square miles had been scanned, and Elliot began the long flight back to Ascension, once again supported by four tankers for a safe arrival at Ascension. The sortie had lasted 14 hours 45 minutes and covered 6,500 miles making it the longest operational reconnaissance sortie in history. The radar prints captured revealed no enemy warships around South Georgia and, equally important, all the northern approaches were free of ice. The Victors would carry out two similar operations before the arrival of the more advanced and appropriately equipped Nimrod. The latter

being delayed while it was hastily converted to be able to accept fuel for its own long-range operations which would be well-supported by the Victor tankers.

V-BOMBER COOPERATION

The series of *Black Buck* operations flown during *Operation Corporate* had bathed the Avro Vulcan in glory (see page 94), but if it was not for the Victor, the world's then-longest bomber raid would not have stood a chance of being successful.

By the end of the Falklands campaign, the tanker force had supported a total of five out of six *Black Buck* operations; *Black Buck 4* was aborted because a pair of tankers were unable to transfer fuel due to an unserviceable Hose Drum Unit (HDU).

SOUTH ATLANTIC COMMITMENT

The Victor tanker force's workload was huge during the Falklands conflict, extending to supporting Nimrod operations, transits of Harrier 'jump-jets' and all-important supply deliveries courtesy of the Hercules. The number of operations took a heavy toll on the future of the Victor fleet and during *Corporate*, crews were flying an average of 120 hours per month compared to just 40 hours in peacetime. Of the 16 aircraft based at Wideawake, on average, 15 of them were tasked every day, the aircraft racking up 3,000 hours of flying time during the campaign on 530 operational sorties and in the process issuing 23 million pounds of fuel! Only three sorties were aborted, and all of these were due to refuelling equipment failures and

not the fault of the aircraft itself. While the commitment eased when the war came to an end on June 14, 1982, the Victor force was kept very busy, the only sign of relief being when the Hercules tanker started to take the strain and Port Stanley airfield was re-opened. It was not until June 10, 1985, when the new Mount Pleasant airfield, capable of receiving all big jets, was opened, that the Victors were stood down and all returned to more peaceful climbs at their Norfolk home.

BUILD UP TO AN UNFORESEEN CONFLICT

The 1980s was a period of steady reduction for the Victor K.2 tanker fleet, beginning with disbandment of 232 OCU in April followed by 57 Squadron on June 30, 1986. All of 57 Squadron's aircraft were transferred to 55 Squadron, the future of which was not predicted to last beyond a few years. However, during a Reconnaissance Air Meet (RAM 90) at Bergstrom AFB near Austin, Texas, where 55 Squadron's Victors were supporting RAF Jaguars, an important recall was issued, ordering the tankers back to Marham. Within 48 hours, 55 Squadron were routing over France and Sicily, refuelling RAF jets being deployed to the Persian Gulf, operating from Punta Raisi in Sicily and RAF Akrotiri in Cyprus. The first to be sent to the Middle East were the Tornado F.3s of 5 and 29 Squadrons based at Coningsby, both regular customers of 55 Squadron whilst performing UK air defence duties.

The catalyst for this action was Saddam Hussein's invasion of its tiny, but oil-rich, neighbour Kuwait on August 2, 1990, which prompted a quick response from the USA. President George H. W. Bush ordered the start of *Operation Desert Shield* five days later to begin preparations to liberate the country.

All Allied air operations were controlled from the HQ Central Command Air Forces (Forward) in Saudi Arabia, a country the Allies were expecting Hussein's forces would attempt to invade next. As such, all priority was aimed at stopping Iraq's huge tank and troop columns which were building on the Saudi border. The Allies were not underestimating Iraq's capability. The country boasted 700 combat aircraft, at least 200 support aircraft, chemical and biological weapons, several types of surface-to-air missiles, approximately 9,000 anti-aircraft guns, and the infamous Scud-B tactical ballistic surface-to-surface missiles it had bought from the Soviet Union. The Iraqi Air Force was formidable too, its aircraft could operate from 24 main airfields plus a further 30 dispersal fields, all of which were well protected by modern, hardened air shelters. Baghdad was the obvious 'hot spot', the Iraqi capital containing 45 high-priority targets making it, at that time, the most heavily defended city in the world.

55 Squadron, under the command of Wing Commander D Williams, had its own priority before joining the theatre. It was tasked with making sure that all the RAF's combat aircraft arrived safely and refuelled Tornado GR.1s, Tornado F.3s, Jaguars, and Buccaneers from their UK and West German stations to their operating bases at Tabuk and Dhahran in Saudi Arabia and Bahrain International Airport (ex-RAF Muharraq). The announcement that the Tornado F.3 would provide air defence cover and the »

Jaguar would also serve as an attack aircraft alongside the Tornado GR.1, was only issued by the MoD on August 9.

Despite all of 55 Squadron's efforts in support of deploying the RAF's forces to the Gulf, to date, only the VC10s of 101 Squadron were operating in the theatre. During a visit to Marham on October 1 by the Commander-in-Chief, Strike Command, Sir 'Paddy' Hines, Wg Cdr Williams was taken aside by the air officer to explain the situation. Williams obviously struggled to hide his disappointment in front of the C-in-C and Hines' parting words, "Your Squadron is highly regarded at High Wycombe, and I know we can count on you if you are needed," did little to make the boss of 55 Squadron feel better and he had serious doubts that the unit would be used at all.

As Christmas 1990 drew closer, a call, came 'out of the blue' from the station commander, Group Captain 'Jock' Stirrup to Williams. Change of plan – four Victors were to deploy to Muharraq, Bahrain in place of four VC10 tankers which were being re-deployed to Saudi Arabia. On December 15, four Victors duly departed Marham bound for Muharraq.

Training continued apace throughout the Christmas period, even on Christmas Day, Wg Cdr Williams being in demand at Strike Command, High Wycombe as the New Year began. To his surprise, a decision had been made to double the Victor detachment to the Gulf.

OPERATION DESERT STORM

The beginning of a huge Allied air campaign began on January 16, 1991, under the name, *Desert Storm.* The RAF's contribution was called *Operation Granby*, and by this time 55 Squadron had been settling in at Muharraq. Of the 2,790 aircraft taking part in the campaign, the RAF contributed 135, of which 46 were Tornado GR.1/1As. The tanker fleet was bolstered by nine 101 Squadron VC10 K.2/3s and a pair of 216 Squadron, Tristar K.1s all operating from King Khalid Airport on the outskirts of Riyadh.

55 Squadron had prepared well for campaign. Before the operation had begun, the unit had been ordered by RAF Strike Command to only support the Jaguar and Tornado F.3 sorties while the VC10 tankers would refuel all the Tornado GR.1 sorties. A great deal of time and effort had gone into allocating 'tow-lines' across Saudi Arabian airspace, but it soon became apparent that such a rigid system would not work in practice and in the end the Victor force refuelled aircraft with a 'probe and drogue' capability from all the Allied air forces. By January 12, 1991, 55 Squadron had declared that they were at a 'war footing' and by January 16, eight Victor K.2s were in theatre ready for action. That afternoon, Wg Cdr Williams along with other Officers Commanding (OCs) of Tornado and Jaguar units were summoned by Group Captain D Henderson (RAF Detachment Commander, Muharraq). It was a short and sweet meeting, Henderson's words leaving

the room deathly silent: "We are going to war tonight; it starts at midnight."

Back at Marham it was the 'norm' to operate mixed crews to spread the experience and flying hours across the squadron. However, for the forthcoming operations aircrew would operate as constituted crews as in, flying with the same team throughout the campaign. The first of those constituted crews to take part was Wg Cdr Williams (navigator) own, made up of the captain, Flight Lieutenant T Hatcher, co-pilot, Flight Lieutenant T Walker and AEO, Flight Lieutenant J Ingham. The sortie would involve a pair of Victor K.2s in support of four Tornados, the tanker providing refuelling on a tow-line path called the 'Olive Low Trail', a route which would be used by 55 Squadron for the entire war. The route was south of the Iraq border, although the final leg turned north, effectively launching the Tornados directly towards their targets without wasting a drop of fuel.

Wg Cdr Williams and his crew walked out to Victor K.2, XM715 *Teasin Tina* at approximately 2200hrs. The aprons were alive at Muharraq with sounds and smells of a wide range of Allied military hardware, all preparing to begin the offensive against Iraq. It was approximately 90 minutes to the Iraqi border from Muharraq; Hussein had been given until midnight to yield to demands and all Allied aircraft were ordered not to cross the border before that time.

At 2250, Flt Lt Hatcher lifted XM715 from Muharraq's main runway and climbed to 9,000ft before setting a course on a westerly track at 300kts. At 2330, they were joined by four Tornado GR.1s armed with JP233s, a very effective anti-runway weapon consisting of 30 bomblets and 215 anti-personnel mines. The Tornados topped up their tanks in total silence and dropped away to low level on a northerly track towards the first of many Iraqi targets while the Victors climbed to 27,000ft and waited for their 'charges' to return. At 0100, all four Tornados reappeared from the darkness, refuelled and the small formation returned safely to Muharraq. It was a similar pattern of operations on January 17, two Victors and four Tornados, this time loaded with 1,000lbs destined for an Iraqi airfield. However, on this occasion, it was clear that something had happened to one of the Tornados and only three returned to

refuel for the trip back to Muharraq. The missing aircraft was crewed by Flight Lieutenant John Peters and Flight Lieutenant John Nichol, the first RAF loss of the war.

Under the control of a Boeing E-3A AWACS, the Victor tankers flew the same or similar route for the entire war, as mentioned, the 'Olive Low Trail', being the most common. All the tow-line routes, except for the ones for the Jaguar force, named *'Puller'* and *'Pusher'* were named after fruits – orange, and lemon, loganberry and prune being some examples. The Buccaneer was added into the mix of tasking from January 26, the force under the command of Wing Commander B Cope playing an important support roll for the Tornados. By this stage, the Victor force had already flown 70 sorties, all without disruption caused by unserviceability and not once was a provided reserve Victor needed to cover a sortie. Serviceability of the Victor K.2 was superb during this period thanks to the dedicated and hard-working groundcrew who kept these aging aircraft flying.

The war only lasted 42 days, ending on February 28, 1991. 55 Squadron had flown 299 sorties during this period, 138 on the 'Olive Low Trail', with an average of 33 sorties per crew. As noted with XM715 *Teasin Tina*, all the Victors were named after the wives of the crew chiefs, complete with impressive artwork carried out by Corporal Andy Price. Five other aircraft were named *Maid Marian* (XH672); *Saucy Sal* (XL164); *Lusty Lindy* (XL231); *Lucky Lou* (XM717) and *Slinky Sue* (XH671) which was changed to *Sweet Sue* as from a distance, 'Slinky' unfortunately looked like 'Stinky'! XL161 and XL190 also took part in the campaign but arrived too late at Muharraq for a christening and nose art to be applied. Mission symbols in the shape of small black petrol pumps were applied to the forward fuselages of all eight aircraft and XM717 also received the profile of a small truck. This 'kill' was credited to XM717 after it struck a lorry and lost a wingtip, whilst taxiing at night at Muharraq.

By March 18, 1991, all of 55 Squadron's Victors were back at Marham, their efficient service keeping the unit busy right up to its disbandment at Marham on September 30, 1993. Thankfully, several of these historic machines are preserved in museums.

RIGHT: **Victor XL161 took part in** *Desert Storm* **but arrived in theatre too late to be adorned with the risqué artwork that most of the unit's aircraft had.**
(Mick Dodsworth)

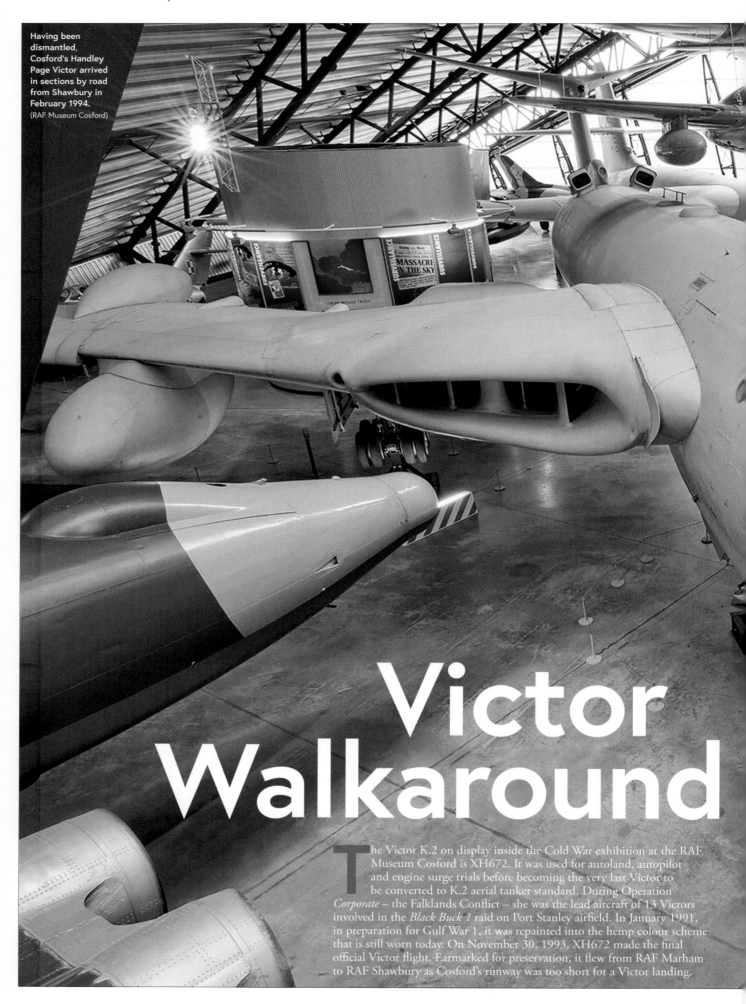

Having been dismantled, Cosford's Handley Page Victor arrived in sections by road from Shawbury in February 1994.
(RAF Museum Cosford)

Victor Walkaround

The Victor K.2 on display inside the Cold War exhibition at the RAF Museum Cosford is XH672. It was used for autoland, autopilot and engine surge trials before becoming the very last Victor to be converted to K.2 aerial tanker standard. During Operation *Corporate* – the Falklands Conflict – she was the lead aircraft of 13 Victors involved in the *Black Buck 1* raid on Port Stanley airfield. In January 1991, in preparation for Gulf War 1, it was repainted into the hemp colour scheme that is still worn today. On November 30, 1993, XH672 made the final official Victor flight. Earmarked for preservation, it flew from RAF Marham to RAF Shawbury as Cosford's runway was too short for a Victor landing.

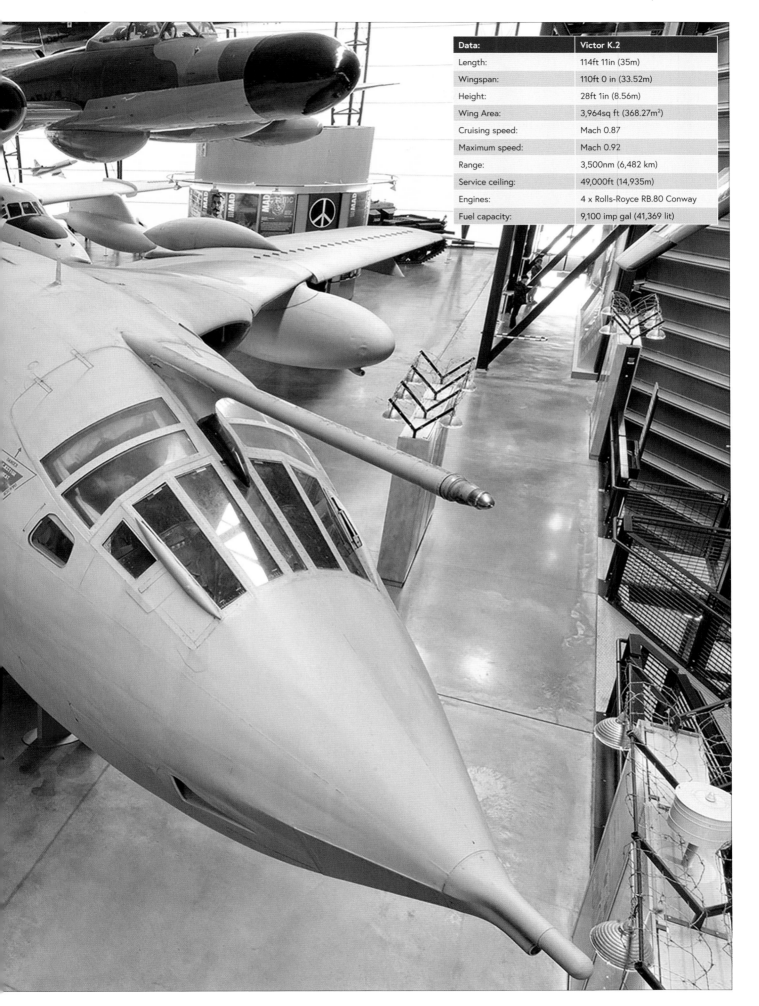

Data:	Victor K.2
Length:	114ft 11in (35m)
Wingspan:	110ft 0 in (33.52m)
Height:	28ft 1in (8.56m)
Wing Area:	3,964sq ft (368.27m²)
Cruising speed:	Mach 0.87
Maximum speed:	Mach 0.92
Range:	3,500nm (6,482 km)
Service ceiling:	49,000ft (14,935m)
Engines:	4 x Rolls-Royce RB.80 Conway
Fuel capacity:	9,100 imp gal (41,369 lit)

Large and permanent fuel tanks were built into the wings of the Victor K.2 variant. (Tom Allett)

The small triangular shaped vents are the NACA intakes, so-called because NASA's predecessor invented their flush-to-the-surface/skin design. One was located on each side of the nose and had a reputation for generating a lot of noise. Small aerodynamic adjustments had made to be made to reduce the amount of disturbance they generated in the cockpit. (Tom Allett)

This image – taken looking back towards the tail of the aircraft – shows the two lights located at the rear of the fuselage that could help to illuminate the centreline drogue during the hours of darkness. The small tyre-link item that lies between them protects the tail from being damaged should over-rotation occur. (Tom Allett)

The port-wing engine air intakes that fed the Rolls-Royce Conway engines. (Tom Allett)

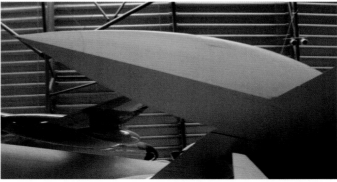

Large trailing edge fairings were added as part of the K.2's redesigned wings. (Tom Allett)

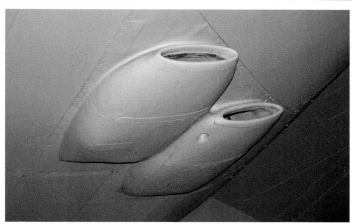

The twin supplementary air intakes that lie directly underneath the main intakes are unique to the Victor K.2 variant. (Tom Allett)

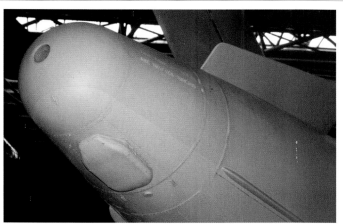

The fuel dump pipe exits via the tail cone on the Victor K.2 variant. (Tom Allett)

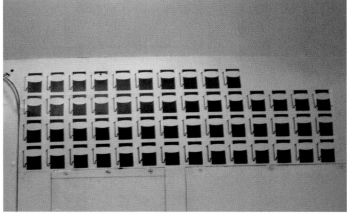

The black petrol pump symbols on XH672's forward fuselage represent the successful air-to-air refuelling sorties it has conducted. XH672 was the 'top scorer' having completed 52 such operations. (Tom Allett)

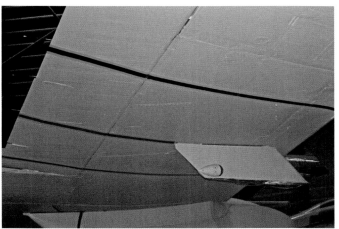

The dayglow-coloured stripes on the wings and rear fuselage helped to guide pilots approaching the trailing basket. (Tom Allett)

The nose undercarriage. Note the X marks which designate the items are no longer serviceable. (Tom Allett)

IN PROFILE

The Victor

VICTOR K.2, XL189, is arguably the most famous Victor of all. Flown by Sqn Ldr Bob Tuxford as 'White 2' during the Falklands War's first Black Buck raid, it was the aircraft that ultimately delivered the fuel that enabled Martin Wither's Vulcan to attack the airfield at Port Stanley.

The crew of XL189 bravely provided more fuel to the Vulcan than it could really spare and other Victor tankers had to be scrambled from Wideawake airfield on the Ascension Island to prevent 189's fuel tanks from running dry over the Atlantic Ocean.

After the airframe was retired from service, she stood on external display for several years. Eventually, this prolonged exposure to the elements damaged the aircraft to the extent that it had to be scrapped.

All profile drawings by
Andrew Hay / flyingart.co.uk

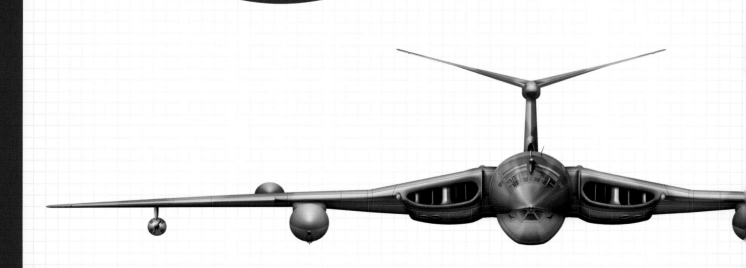

The Victor in Miniature

Andy Davies' build of an Airfix 1:72 Victor depicts K.2, XH673, of 57 Squadron which was built as a Mk B.2 bomber variant and later converted to the airborne tanker role. She is depicted in the grey/green camouflage she wore while serving with the Victor Training Flight at RAF Wittering. Note how the kit was built with the flaps in the down position while the airbrakes and crew door are open.

The real XH673 survived a wheels-up landing on foam at RAF Waddington in March 1962 following an in-flight hydraulic failure but was repaired and returned to service.

After the RAF's Victor fleet was retired in 1993, XH673, by then painted in an overall desert Hemp colour scheme, became RAF Marham's 'gate guard'. Her many years outdoors eventually took their toll and the aircraft's structure deteriorated to the extent that she had to be dismantled in November-December 2020. Much of the airframe was scrapped. (AMW - Andy Davies)

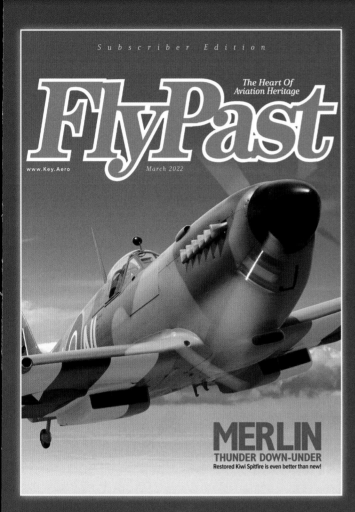

The True Delta Ladies

Chris Pierce recalls the development of the prototype Type 698s, VX770 and VX777. Their advance design brought a striking new shape to the sky.

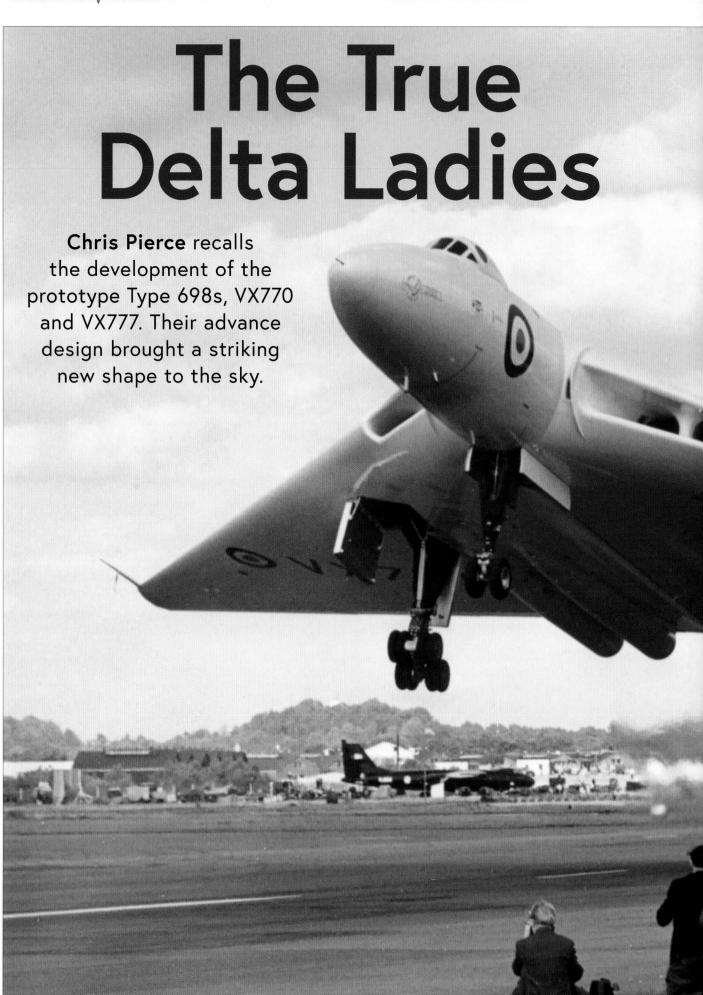

It took Avro just 28 months to construct one of the country's most advanced bomber designs. The first of two prototype 698s, VX770 was rolled out at Woodford on August 30, 1952. In a brilliant all-gloss white paint scheme, only broken up by its large RAF roundels and fin flashes, the big delta would have made a very impressive sight. In the capable hands of Avro's Chief Test Pilot, Wg Cdr R J 'Roly' Falk, VX770 was taxied out onto Woodford's main runway where he conducted several high-speed taxi runs to get a feel for the controls and check all the systems were working correctly. VX770 was fitted with the very minimum of systems required for flight and this meant that there was no requirement for a co-pilot or supporting crew. Falk was on his own and before he committed to the aircraft's historic first flight, he made a final high-speed run to test the all-important brakes and make sure the nose wheel steering was not shimmying. Now convinced that the Type 698 was ready to fly, Falk had to wait patiently at the end of the runway while some reluctant birds were moved on. Now clear, Falk opened the throttles of the four Rolls Royce RA.3 Avon turbojets of just 6,500lb each and VX770 made a short roll down the runway before taking to the air. The gear was retracted after a short climb and Flak continued upwards to 10,000ft; the limit of the aircraft's operational ceiling owing to a lack of cockpit pressurisation. A series of gentle manoeuvres were conducted before Falk began a steady descent back down to Woodford. Once over the airfield, Falk lowered the undercarriage at which point air traffic control reported that they had seen something fall from the aircraft. Nothing untoward was being indicated to Falk but as a precaution he remained in the circuit while a Vampire and a Type 707 joined him to make a visual check of the aircraft. Both pilots spotted that each of the main undercarriage leg fairings were missing. The problem was a cosmetic one and with the mystery solved, Falk lined VX770 up for landing which he conducted safely, deploying the aircraft's giant brake parachute to reduce the wear on the brakes.

There was now a race for VX770 to complete the required number of flying hours so it could perform at that year's SBAC show at Farnborough. This was achieved, although the classified nature of the aircraft meant that Falk had to fly VX770 from Boscombe Down as it was not cleared to land at Farnborough. Several flypasts were made during the show, including one where the Avro 707A, WD280 and 707B, VX790 provided a very impressive escort. »

MAIN PICTURE:
Avro's Type 698s were officially given the Vulcan name in September 1952.
(KEY Archive)

V IS FOR VULCAN

It was now time to officially name the beast, Avro having already suggested the name 'Ottawa' in keeping with the bomber tradition of naming them after towns and cities within the British Empire. However, Vickers had already named their Type 660 the Valiant and the Chief of Air Staff, Sir John Slessor, stated that he wanted the remaining two aircraft to have names beginning with the same initial. So, in late September 1952, the Type 698 was given the name Vulcan and, by the end of the year, the H.P.80 was named the Victor.

After its brief public outing, VX770 spent several weeks in a hangar at Woodford being brought up to a more purposeful specification. Modifications included the fitment of an ejection seat for the co-pilot, revised pilots' instrument panels, air-conditioning and a pressurisation system. Up until then the aircraft had been flown with its fuel tanks temporally fitted in the bomb bay. Now the tanks were fitted in their appropriate positions in the wings along with the maze of plumbing required. By the end of October 1952, the work was completed and VX770 was back in the air.

By January 1953 and with 32 flying hours under her belt, it was apparent that the RA.3 Avon engines were not pushing the aircraft anywhere near its full potential. The aircraft had always been designed with the more

powerful Bristol Olympus in mind, but these were still not available. As a stop gap, VX770 was resigned to the hangar floor again, this time to be fitted with four Armstrong Siddeley Sapphire SA.6 turbojets, each developing a more respectable 7,500lb of thrust. This was still well short of the planned 10,000lb of thrust that the Olympus engines were promising. Several other systems were revised before flight testing began again in July.

SECOND PROTOTYPE

While VX770 continued its trials, the second prototype, VX777, was taking shape at Woodford. Several subtle, but important changes were incorporated into the second prototype, all of which brought it closer to the final production variant. These included a longer nose leg and in turn a longer undercarriage bay to accommodate it. It was discovered during the Type 707 trials that by raising the angle of attack of the wing up by 3.5°, the length of the take off run was significantly reduced. Many other systems were changed and improved, and the bomb aimer's blister was also fitted under the nose. However, the most significant change of all was the engines, which initially were four Bristol Olympus Mk.99s that had been fitted to conduct engine ground runs and the myriad of electrical system checks. These were replaced by four

Olympus Mk.100s, each developing 9,750lb of thrust as the aircraft was prepared for its first flight. This came on September 3, 1953, and the now traditional rush to make that year's SBAC was once again achieved. As well as performing flypasts of its own during the Farnborough Air Show, VX777 was also joined by VX770 and, during one particularly memorable flypast, was also joined by four Type 707s.

Back to work, VX777 continued its own test flying programme with Avro – and later – the Aeroplane and Armament Experimental Establishment (A&AEE) at Boscombe Down. Further testing revealed several engine problems, one of which was RPM creep at altitude which could lead to an alarming increase in the jet pipe temperatures (JPT). This problem was partially attributed to the flexing of the airframe which upset the long throttle control runs. The problem was solved by fitting a cruise governor which allowed full power on take-off but once airborne, the throttle was restricted below the maximum.

Tests at the A&AEE revealed a tendency for the port-inner engine to surge which, after much investigation, was found to be caused by how the air was entering the intake. After several methods were tried, a detent system was applied to both inboard engines which improved the handling of the aircraft ten-fold.

The A&AEE also had at its disposal a ground rig, supplied by Avro, which consisted of a port intake, a section of the wing and a 10ft piece of the forward fuselage. Continuous ground runs could now be made at leisure, initially concentrating on the way the intake behaved in conjunction with the fuel system. After reaching a successful conclusion, the test rig was then used for trials on the siting of the various engine accessories and their cooling. One problem that was encountered in the air but not the test rig, was when the engine intake's anti-icing

system would overheat the oil tank housed in the intakes main partition, or bullet. A redesign of the oil cooling system soon rectified this. The test rig did reveal that the pitot head, in contrast, tended to ice up and this was also moved into the bullet and another problem was logically solved.

TRIAL AFTER TRIAL

On July 14, 1954, VX777 was transferred to the Royal Aircraft Establishment (RAE) to be prepared for the Vulcan's main role of dropping bombs. Unfortunately, this latest trial would have to be postponed because, on July 27, VX777 was declared as Category 3 damaged following the loss of rudder control. With Falk at the controls, a very hard rudder manoeuvre was conducted which caused the control surface to stay locked in that position. Unable to see what was going on, the crew presumed that, at best, it and a section of the fin had been torn off, but a low pass of the Farnborough control tower confirmed that all was still intact. A very delicate landing followed, using asymmetric power to counter the effect of the jammed rudder. Once on the ground, there was little chance of stopping the bomber from overshooting the runway and sinking into the soft ground causing a partial undercarriage collapse. Unable to exit via the crew door, Flak had to release the canopy manually as it had not yet been fitted with the standard explosive bolts. While holding the canopy up, the crew evacuated the aircraft before Flak left the stricken bomber. To recover the Vulcan, deep trenches had to be dug to help the lifting equipment get underneath. Once free, the undercarriage was locked down and fixed so that the aircraft could be flown back to Woodford for repairs. The engineers quickly found the rudder problem was caused by a failed Powered Flying Control Unit (PFCU). Even though ❯❯

RIGHT: The initial configuration of the first prototype Vulcan, VX770, was changed. Its original Avon engines were just an interim installation, while the wing was subject to significant alteration. (KEY Archive)

this was backed up by a secondary PFCU, the rudder had jammed at such an angle it had gone beyond the operating limit of both units. The system was modified so it would never occur again. While at Woodford, Avro took the opportunity to fit another set of engines, this time it was the Olympus 101 producing 11,000lbs of thrust which would become the standard engine for the future Vulcan B.1, the first of which, XA899, had already made its maiden flight on February 4, 1955.

Avro's own flight development trials were resumed on March 23, 1955, although this was destined to be a brief exercise. VX777 was transferred to the A&AEE for preview trials on March 30, although all maintenance for the aircraft was still the responsibility of Avro back at Woodford. This was a busy period for the second prototype which was certainly put through its paces at Boscombe Down. There, 17 flights totalling 72 flying hours were achieved before the aircraft was returned to Avro in late May 1955. The A&AEE flights had been flown at weights between 119,000lb and 130,000lb, although the actual operational weight of the Vulcan was going to be in the region of 165,000lb. The trials were also flown at just Mach 0.87 when the production B.1s were planned to fly at Mach 0.95. Alarmingly, test pilots discovered that when the aircraft reached Mach 0.86 the Vulcan tended to pitch down and this increased as speed was gained. This obviously made the aircraft very difficult to fly accurately and within the speed limitations set by the Avro. Additionally, the ailerons had problems of their own because of a looseness in the hinges, which caused an oscillation effect at higher speeds which in turn restricted manoeuvrability. Avro was aware of all these problems and was already developing an auto Mach trimmer and pitch dampener to rectify the higher speed problems. More significantly, a completely new wing was being designed which would solve all the early Vulcan's problems in virtually one go.

Following this latest A&AEE trial, it was concluded that VX777, in its current form, was not acceptable as a high-altitude bomber. Aside from all the speed and flight problems encountered, the aircraft could only carry a 10,000lb bomb load up to 43,000ft. This was far too low for a modern bomber, even at night. The aircraft was praised by the A&AEE staff for having many outstanding features, but they had to conclude that the Vulcan, in this form, would not be considered for RAF service.

Thankfully, the prototypes, like the Avro 707s before them were being overtaken by more advanced versions.

Meanwhile, VX770 had continued to carry out valuable trials throughout 1955 working with both Avro and the A&AEE. On June 8, 1956, the aircraft was back at Woodford to begin a special trial to fly with a set of Rolls-Royce Conways. VX770 was fitted with four RCo.7 engines of which a later version was destined to power the Handley Page Victor. By August 9, 1957, VX770 was transferred to Rolls-Royce so it could conduct its own trials on the new powerful engine installation. With all this surplus power compared to the earlier Avons, new flight envelopes could be pursued allowing the Vulcan to fly higher and faster than before. Like the A&AEE test pilots, the Avro crews experienced the same problems with buffet and pitching between Mach 0.80 and 0.85 which could only be solved in the short term by flying lower and slower than the aircraft was designed for. The aerodynamicists discovered that the problem lay with the airflow across the upper surfaces, which split, causing a compressibility stall. The Type 707 was brought in to help resolve the problem with wing fences and vortex generators being fitted. While this did not solve the problem it did highlight how to resolve it which could only be achieved by redesigning the entire leading edge of the wing. The original straight-edged delta had a sweep of 52°, but after extensive wind tunnel testing at Farnborough it was found that the solution was to be found by introducing a cranked inner section. It was angled at 42° while the outer section retained the 52° sweep. A slight droop was also introduced to the outer section which in turn increased the chord of the wing, raised the lift coefficient, therefore lifting the compressibility buffet way beyond the speed of the aircraft.

This new Phase Two C or Mk.2 wing was first fitted to VX777 which first took to the air in its new form on October 5, 1955. Initial flight trials were successful, and the new shape of the Vulcan was first seen by the public at Farnborough in 1957. VX770 was also in the planning for the Phase Two wing, but a tragic accident would occur before the work could be carried out.

TRAGIC LOSS

During the morning of September 20, 1958, VX770 was being prepared at Hucknall for another test flight relating to its Conway engines. If all the trials set for the sortie that day were carried out with time to spare,

LEFT: **After the loss of the first prototype VX770 at the 1958 RAF Syerston At Home air display, VX777 continued to serve as a trials aircraft until February 1962.** (KEY Archive)

ABOVE: **Delta jet heaven! The first two Vulcan prototypes, VX770 and VX777, flying in formation with the Avro 707s during the 1953 SBAC show at Farnborough. The 707s were all painted different colours — blue, red, orange and silver.**
(KEY Archive)

the plan was to make a low flypast at the nearby RAF Syerston Battle of Britain Air Display. The crew on this flight were all Rolls-Royce employees, except for the navigator, Flt Lt Ray Parrott. The remainder of the crew consisted of the pilot, Keith Sturt, the co-pilot Ronald Ford (seconded from Fairey Aviation) and the flight engineer, William Howkins. With their tasking completed, Sturt approached Syerston for a brief display at approximately 1300hrs GMT. It is known that Sturt intended flying at 250ft at a speed between 200 and 300kts down runway 07 before completing his display and returning to Hucknall. Witnesses claim the aircraft was flying nearer to 350kts or Mach 0.61 when it approached the airfield from the west, which would be still well within the aircraft's safe operating speed. During the pass, Sturt made a rate one turn to starboard at which point, the starboard wing's leading edge began to fail at the point where it joins the centre section. It rapidly peeled back, destroying the entire wing within seconds. As the bomber continued onwards trailing huge clouds of vapourising fuel, it pitched towards the ground, before rising to an almost vertical attitude. At this point the bomber slipped earthwards, engulfed in flames, before

scattering itself along the end of runway 07 in a trail of destruction measuring over 1,400 yards. The four crew perished along with three other RAF servicemen, Sgt C Hanson, Sgt E D Simpson, and SAC J J Tonks, who were on the ground manning the airfield controller's caravan. There is much conjecture that continues today about the exact cause of this accident although the popular and official viewpoint is that the aircraft exceeded the limits imposed on the aircraft. This may have been the case, but the amount of punishing trials work that VX770 had been put through since its first flight must have taken its toll on the airframe and could have contributed to such a catastrophic failure of the wing.

VX777 was allocated to the RAE again on April 17, 1960, this time to conduct ground vibration trials of various equipment, including the armament installation. Ten days later, further trials continued at Farnborough, but this was destined to be the last act for VX777. It was withdrawn from use on February 7, 1962 and was struck off charge on October 18 that year. Quickly falling into a semi-derelict state, the second prototype was stripped of any useful spares and, with no ceremony, was scrapped at Farnborough in July 1963.

Confidence was understandably high when Vulcan XA897 was en route to London Airport (LAP – now known as Heathrow) after undertaking a highly successful flag-waving trip to the other side of the globe.

The giant delta-winged bomber was the first of its type to be delivered to the RAF and was effectively put on show to the world – especially potential enemies – during its marathon 26,000-mile journey.

XA897 was the ninth production Vulcan and was officially handed over to the RAF at Waddington on July 20, 1956, to become part of the newly formed 230 Operational Conversion Unit (OCU). However, its stay was short-lived, and the bomber was soon returned to Avro's Woodford factory for a series of modifications prior to taking part in a long-range promotional flight to New Zealand. Although promoted as a goodwill flight, the real aim was to emphasise that Britain now had a nuclear strike capability that could effectively reach anywhere in the world. It would also give the RAF a great opportunity to find and ultimately resolve any teething problems with the new aircraft type that were revealed along the way.

The aircraft's captain for the New Zealand trip was Squadron Leader Donald Howard while the commander-in-chief of Bomber Command no less, Air Marshal Sir Harry Broadhurst, took the co-pilot's seat. Although the Vulcan was brand new to the RAF the outbound flight, via Aden, Singapore, and Melbourne, was completed without any significant problems with a journey time – including stopovers – of 47 hours and 26 minutes. From there the aircraft visited Sydney and Adelaide before moving on Christchurch, arriving on September 18, thereby giving huge kudos to the RAF, Avro, Rolls-Royce, and the British government.

RETURN JOURNEY

The return journey routed via Brisbane, Darwin, Singapore, Ceylon, and Aden. The flight was airborne at 0250 on October 1, but instead of heading for Waddington it headed for London. XA897 was to be the focal point of a VIP reception that had been set up at London Airport, where representatives from the RAF, Avro, the Ministry of Aviation, and the crew's family members would meet the aircraft on arrival. Unsurprisingly, the national and local media were there in force. Unfortunately, as the Vulcan approached the coast of the English Channel, the weather reports for their intended destination were dreadful with driving rain and complete and thick cloud cover at 700ft, with a further 'two eights' cloud at 300ft. Nevertheless, the Vulcan's crew continued their approach above the cloud and Howard radioed Bomber Command's headquarters at High Wycombe for updates.

Meanwhile, the airport's scheduled flights continued to arrive with the assistance of a ground controller's 'talk down' but three airline crews had chosen to divert because of the poor weather. Officially, Squadron Leader Howard who was designated as the aircraft's commander, considered diverting the flight to Waddington, where the weather was significantly better but chose to keep heading for London. but it is not known whether the hugely influential senior officer sitting next to him was really 'calling the shots'.

Rather than disappointing the gathered crowd, the crew pressed ahead for London.

They began to descend into the gloom, entering an instrument approach with five nautical miles to run before touchdown at 1,500 feet. Spectators gathered on top of the Queen's Building ventured out, determined to brave the elements to see the Vulcan's arrival. The GCA talk-down began as normal with the glide path and centreline corrections being issued verbally from a radar controller until the aircraft was 3/4 of a mile from the runway at which point the ground controller instructed the captain that he was now 80ft above the glide path.

The subsequent investigation determined that this was the last elevation advice received from the controller and just a few seconds after that exchange, the Vulcan's extended landing gear smashed into the ground. Due to the dreadful weather, the first idea the assembled crowd had of the Vulcan's proximity, was a sudden roar ≫

The funeral pyre of the RAF's first Vulcan. On October 1, 1957, B.1 XA897 was returning from a triumphant tour of Australia and New Zealand when it crashed on approach to London (now Heathrow) Airport. The pilots ejected but the four other crew were killed. (KEY Archive)

Triumph and Tragedy

Just as the Vulcan was emerging as a world-beating aircraft, disaster struck. **Tom Allett** explains.

of its engines as the Vulcan's four Olympus engines wound-up to full power. It then shot into view, climbing steeply away from the runway. As the aircraft passed through 800ft the cockpit canopy was jettisoned and the pilots followed just a couple of seconds later.

The aircraft, now being completely out of control, rolled sharply to starboard before entering a 30° descent back to the runway where it smashed into the ground and exploded in a huge ball of flame. The four crew members still inside the aircraft,

Squadron Leader Stroud (Howard's regular co-pilot who was in the aircraft's radar navigator's seat), Squadron Leader Eames, Squadron Leader Gamble, and Mr Frederick Bassett from the Avro company had obviously been killed instantly but the crash rescue teams continued to battle the blaze for almost an hour. There was nothing more that they could do.

Amongst those looking upon the devastation was Avro's chief aerodynamicist Roy Ewans. Looking at the shattered wreckage he noticed that the main undercarriage legs were nowhere to be seen. He started to walk and then drive one of airport vehicles along the aircraft's debris route but even after passing about 300 yards of wreckage, he still could not see any trace of the main undercarriage.

He then drove outside of the airport boundary and started searching the field that lay under the Vulcan's approach to the runway where he subsequently found two deep holes that were already filling with rainwater. He concluded that the Vulcan's main undercarriage must have made the holes when it had momentarily hit the ground. When measured, it was discovered that the aircraft first made contact with the grass field 1,988ft (606m) short of the runway, displaced to the north by approximately 250ft. Ahead of the impact holes were two patches of vegetables that had been flattened by the bomber's jet blast as the aircraft began to climb away. The main wheels themselves were found strewn across the field.

Even though the Vulcan's undercarriage was built to take the weight of bumpy touchdowns, it could not be expected to survive a heavy impact with a muddy field. Nevertheless, despite the loss of the aircraft's lower undercarriage leg assembly, that alone would not be expected to cause the aircraft to crash. Unfortunately, the huge backward-facing force caused by hitting the ground had also caused the undercarriage's drag struts to fail, which allowed the mainwheel legs to be hurled backward, smashing into the underside of the wing in front of the trailing edge control surfaces. The undercarriage punctured the wing just at the spot where the aileron control rods were located, wrecking them, thereby removing all lateral control of the aircraft. From that moment, disaster was inevitable.

The formal investigations began the very next day when an RAF Court of Inquiry chaired by Air Chief Marshal Sir Donald Hardman was opened. On October 26, the minister of transport and civil aviation asked Dr I G Touch, director of electronics research and development at the Ministry of Supply to conduct an independent accident investigation with a particular focus upon the standards

and procedures used by the airport's ground controlled approach (GCA) facilities. Dr Touch concluded within his report: "The Ground Controlled Approach equipment was correctly set up and calibrated and there is no evidence of malfunctioning or failure. The controller failed to warn the pilot of his closeness to the ground. During the last ten seconds of the approach the aircraft made a steep descent to the ground. The cause for this descent was probably due to the build-up of oscillations about the glide path.

"Poor talk-down by the controller contributed to things, but as the approach was subject to the overriding judgement of the pilot, the controller was not to blame for events arising from the control.

"The critical phase was the first four seconds after the descent steepened, during which no height guidance was given to the pilot.

"It is very difficult to pass judgement on this matter but in view of all the circumstances I do not think the controller should be blamed. No warning was given during the final five or six seconds. It should have been, although it would have been too late.

"Although it cannot definitely be proven, the most likely theory is that the controller made an error of judgement concentrating too much upon azimuthal correctional and paying insufficient attention to the elevation error meter.

"Human errors are more likely to occur under stress or unusual circumstances. In my opinion evidence exists to show the all the elements in the GCA servo chain were strained."

Dr Touch went on to explain that the term 'servo-chain' referred to how the pilot reacted to the GCA information, describing the cycle of events as a kind of 'mutual loop' between the pilot and the ground controller.

The post-accident technical investigation that formed part of the RAF court of inquiry stated that the aircraft had "not suffered any technical failures" and "was perfectly serviceable at the point of initial impact."

The inquiry determined that the Vulcan's captain had "made an error of judgement in selecting an unsuitable break-off height of 300ft" and had been "unwise to then go below that height still out of visual contact with the ground."

The ground controller warned the captain that he was 80ft above the glidepath just seven seconds before hitting the ground, but no subsequent warning was given when the aircraft rapidly went below the glidepath. Astonishingly, the talk down had continued after the Vulcan had first hit the ground, as if the approach were still continuing normally.

Consequently, the RAF inquiry decided that the failure to warn the pilot that he was below the glidepath was the primary cause of the accident. This was a slightly different decision from that made by Dr Touch, but as it was RAF policy not to make court of inquiry evidence public, Touch would not have known what the RAF had concluded.

At the inquest into the deaths of the four men seated in the rear crew seats, it was highlighted that another contributing cause was an altimeter error.

In his summing up, the coroner, Dr H Broadbridge, said there was nothing in the evidence to show criminal negligence on the part of anyone in the aircraft or on the ground, adding "everyone seemed to be doing their duty as they thought appropriate at the time. Despite several investigations and a number of theories being put forward, no single factor has ever been identified as the principal cause of XA897's tragic accident."

Today, the four men lost in the London Airport crash, Sqn Ldr Stroud, Sqn Ldr Eames, Sqn Ldr Gamble, and Frederick Bassett from the Avro company, rest next to each other in a cemetery at Waddington village, a short distance from where the RAF's mighty Vulcans once howled. One can only imagine their thoughts after the shock of the initial crash impact, then hearing the bangs of their pilots' ejection seat which confirmed their last chance of survival had gone.

BELOW: Vulcan B.1s from the first production batch of 25. The first six production Vulcans (XA889–XA894) were used for various trials during the type's development programme. (KEY Archive)

"Although it cannot definitely be proven, the most likely theory is that the controller made an error of judgement concentrating too much upon azimuthal correctional and paying insufficient attention to the elevation error meter."

- Dr I G Touch, director of electronics research and development at the Ministry of Supply

A TTENTION, ATTENTION, this is the bomber controller, for bomb list Sierra, SCRAMBLE…I repeat…for bomb list Sierra, SCRAMBLE, SCRAMBLE."

If you heard such a tannoy announcement for real at an RAF airfield in the 1950s or '60s, the speed of your reaction during the next three to ten minutes might just save your life. Should the Soviet Union launch a pre-emptive strike against the UK it was estimated that NATO radars could only give a maximum of 15 minutes notice of inbound Russian ballistic missiles and the airfields accommodating Britain's V-force nuclear deterrent might receive no more than ten minutes warning of their imminent destruction.

Thankfully, the well-drilled and precise instructions of the bomber controller, the RAF duty officer responsible for launching Britain's nuclear bombers for a retaliatory strike on the Soviet Union, were never used for real, but they were repeatedly practised.

The idea of the RAF having aircraft on permanent standby to intercept enemy raiders stretched back to World War One. By 1962 this practice, whether for defending fighters or retaliating nuclear bombers was called Quick Reaction Alert (QRA). The Bomber Command airfields that held nuclear QRA status – the practice of having armed nuclear bombers on permanent standby around the clock – were the backbone of Britain's deterrent capabilities until the »

Wargames

The RAF repeatedly honed the skills of its nuclear bomber crews at home and overseas. **Tom Allett** reports.

"ATTENTION, ATTENTION, this is the bomber controller, for bomb list Sierra, SCRAMBLE...for bomb list Sierra, SCRAMBLE, SCRAMBLE."

ABOVE: **Should the worst happen... After nearly a decade of tests and development, Avro's** *Blue Steel* **nuclear stand-off weapon was introduced into RAF service in February 1963. Here an 83 Squadron Vulcan carrying a** *Blue Steel* **bomb recessed in its bomb bay, awaits the Armageddon call.** (KEY Archive)

BELOW: **A 617 Squadron Vulcan blasts off during a scramble exercise at Scampton on August 26, 1960. At one point, the idea of using the Vulcan as carrier aircraft for three Folland Gnats was discussed, but it never progressed.** (KEY Archive)

RAF transferred its nuclear shield to the Royal Navy's *Polaris* submarines in 1968. The RAF continually practised V-force scrambles. The aim was to keep the time between the scramble call and the aircrafts' wheels leaving the ground under the three-minute mark – easier said than done. However, the RAF was not always the defender in such exercises, it also routinely played the attacking enemy force when simulating air attacks for air defence training purposes.

When the Vulcan first entered service, its performance simply outclassed many of the jet fighter aircraft of the day. Its speed and service ceiling put it beyond the reach of many potential adversaries. With such a special weapon entering its armoury, it is no surprise that the RAF was keen to show just how effective the aircraft was.

The perfect opportunity to demonstrate the then new Vulcan's capabilities against a modern fighter force came via a series of US air defence exercises call *Sky Shield* (I-IV) which the RAF was invited to take part in. *Sky Shield 1* (SS1) took place in September 1960 and set the precedent for shutting down all commercial and general aviation flights that operated in the 'combat zone' exercise area. This allowed the participating forces the opportunity to fly as they would during a real strike, without the risk of colliding with passenger aircraft. That July, the US authorities gave airlines operating in North America eight weeks' notice that a large military air defence exercise would take place

and asked them to adjust their schedules accordingly. It was estimated that about 1,000 US commercial flights and 700 general aviation aircraft movements were affected by SS1 in some way. Canada also joined the exercise, meaning that around a further 310 flights were affected. It took more than two months of planning to prepare for the unprecedented exercise, but it was as realistic as could be within a training exercise.

United States Air Force (USAF) B-47 Stratojet and B-52 Stratofortress nuclear bombers from Strategic Air Command would be joined by eight RAF Vulcans, all tasked with evading the USAF's defending fighter force and reaching a potential worthy target, which were primarily airfields.

The RAF's plan called for its force to be divided in two. Four would attack from the north (Scotland) while the remainder would approach from the south (Bermuda). All 'survivors' were to fly to Newfoundland and Labrador and land at Earnest Harman Air Force Base, Stephenville.

The Vulcans' 'survival' chances would, as usual, partly depend on the jet's envious speed and manoeuvrability, but the RAF bombers had another 'ace' up their sleeve – an electronic countermeasures (ECM) system that would attempt to jam the USAF's ground and airborne radars.

The Vulcans replicated the expected attack profile of Russian bombers and approached from the highest altitude – around 55-56,000ft – while the B-47s and B-52s flew at medium and lower altitudes, some as low as 500ft.

The first 'kill' of the exercise was achieved by a defending F-101 Voodoo jet fighter which 'shot down' a Vulcan 56,000ft above Goose Bay, on Canada's eastern coast. Nevertheless, the remaining seven British bombers were all able to avoid the defending fighters and complete their tasks. All seven 'survivors' were all able to touch-down unscathed in Newfoundland and Labrador, thereby completing an unprecedented display of air power. Imagine the celebrations at Bomber Command's headquarters! By comparison, all the participating B-47s and B-52s were 'shot down'.

The US authorities deemed the exercise a success and it set the precedent for the rest of the series.

SKY SHIELD II

Sky Shield II (SS II), scheduled for October 14-15, 1961, was a far larger affair. It comprised approximately 250 bombers tasked with attacking the same number of missile sites which were to be defended by some 1,800 fighter

ABOVE: **During the US** *Sky Shield II* **exercise, the Vulcan's manoeuvrability and electronic countermeasure capabilities put its potential survivability above that of the USAF's legendary B-52 bomber.** (72nd Air Base Wing Public Affairs USAF)

aircraft from more than 50 US fighter units. The defending fleet included some of the best interceptors of the day such as the McDonnell F-101 Voodoo; Convair F-102 Delta Dagger and F-106 Delta Dart; Lockheed F-14 Starfighter, Northrop F-89J Scorpion and Douglas F4D Skyray. More than 200,000 service personnel participated including representatives from North American Aerospace Defense Command (NORAD), the US Army, Navy and Air Force, the Air National Guard, Royal Air Force and Royal Canadian Air Force.

Again, the RAF was keen to pit its Vulcans and their electronic countermeasures against the US and Canadian air forces and once more lined-up eight of its giant delta-wing jets to participate. Four were supplied by 27 Squadron, flying from Kindley Air Force Base in Bermuda with the other four provided by 83 Squadron operating from RAF Kinloss, Scotland. Again, the Vulcans – approaching from north and south – represented the Russian attack profile, flying at 56,000ft, while the USAF B-52 operated between 35-42,000ft and the B-47s performed the low-level tasks.

This time the RAF bombers changed tactics, using three from each formation to put up an ECM 'shield' while the fourth aircraft would disengage and attempt to slip away to the target while the defending fighters concentrated their efforts on the ECM providers. Again, the Vulcans won the day. A 27 Squadron aircraft flying from Bermuda – assisted by its teammates' electronic jamming efforts - dodged the defenders and headed north, landing – perhaps embarrassingly for the Americans – at Plattsburgh Air Force Base, New York. Had the Vulcan been a Russian machine, the great city was open to destruction. The northern Vulcan force adopted a stream attack – flying in a line, one behind another – and completed their tasks having reported only a single radar contact from an intercepting fighter during their entire journey. Of course, risk can never be fully eliminated from flying duties, even during exercises and a sad footnote to *Sky Shield II* is that a USAF B-52 crashed into the Atlantic with the loss of eight lives.

Despite the fatal accident, USAF General Laurence Kuter, the US commander of the operation, was quoted in numerous media reports as saying the event was "the greatest exercise in information analysis, decision-making and action-taking in continental aerospace defence in all

BELOW: **An F-101 Voodoo was the only aircraft type to score a 'kill' against a Vulcan during the US** *Sky Shield* **air defence exercises of the 1960s.** (KEY Archive)

our history," but refused requests for him to 'score' the teams involved claiming *Sky Shield's* objective was "by no means a contest between offensive and defensive forces."

After studying the post-exercise results, a detailed report was compiled and stashed away in top secret archives. Some parts remain classified, but most of the findings entered the public domain in 1997, when the Vulcans' success was revealed. Indeed, the interceptors' performance had been shaky overall, as it was concluded that almost 50% of the 'enemy' aircraft inbound at low-level were not detected and of those that were temporarily identified some 40% then thwarted the radar tracking with evasive manoeuvres. The report summarised that no more than a quarter of the attacking bombers in *Sky Shield II* would have been shot down and in theory, the cities of New York, Washington DC and Chicago could all have been destroyed before the Vulcans ran out of fuel.

The remaining two *Sky Shield* exercises were quite different from their predecessors, using different aircraft types to evaluate various aspects of the North American defences. *Sky Shield II* remains one of the largest air operations ever performed by the western allies and while RAF Vulcans would go on to achieve considerable success in later generations of US exercises such as *Red Flag*, *Sky Shield* surely provided one of the Vulcan's 'finest hours' in peacetime.

Conventional Conversion

By comparison to submarines, aircraft are vulnerable delivery vehicles which meant the Vulcans left nuclear service and returned to conventional roles.

BELOW: **Vulcan B.2, XM575, of 44 Squadron, seconds from touchdown at RAF Waddington. Note the extended air brakes above the wings.** (KEY Archive)

That old saying, time stands still for no man, is equally true for machines. Despite its enduring 'space age' looks, the successful development of anti-aircraft missiles eventually made all V-force aircraft obsolescent in the high-altitude nuclear strike role. The Vulcan's days as part of Britain's nuclear deterrent were numbered the moment that USAF U-2 pilot, Gary Powers, was shot down over Russia. His aircraft was brought down by an SA-2 Guideline surface-to-air missile while operating at 70,000ft. The date was May 1, 1960.

If the U-2 could not avoid air defences when flying 13 miles above the ground, neither could any V-force aircraft who were limited to altitudes in the region of 50-55,000ft.

The Powers' incident led the RAF to re-train for low-level airspace penetrations, but it was soon accepted that the potency of the Soviet Union's missile defences – and the possibility that the V-force could be destroyed on their airfield by a pre-emptive strike – meant the nuclear deterrent role must pass to the far-less vulnerable Royal Navy Polaris submarines that would begin their first nuclear patrol on June 30, 1969.

The 'post-Powers' introduction of low-level flying proved to be the downfall of the Vickers Valiant when metal fatigue issues developed and made the repair costs uneconomical. The Victor and Vulcan fleets were successfully adapted to the low-level bombing role and both fleets swapped their

LEFT: XL318, now resident at the RAF Museum, Hendon, is seen over the Fylingdales 'golf ball' radars (since changed for a different design) that have been a crucial element of the UK's missile early warning and surveillance system since 1963.
(KEY Archive)

LEFT: After ending their strategic nuclear bombing role, the Vulcan and Victor fleets swapped their all-white anti-flash colours for the grey/green camouflage needed for the low-level attack role. Here, XM597 is pictured trailing her tail parachute on May 31, 1973.
(KEY Archive)

BELOW: Avro Vulcan B.2, XM609, blasts away from RAF Waddington on May 8, 1975.
(KEY Archive)

all-white anti-flash markings for grey/green camouflage on their upper surfaces, the first being redelivered to the RAF in the new colours in 1964. Some Victors were converted to perform valuable service in the maritime reconnaissance role but, eventually, concerns about the fatigue effect upon the Victor airframes led to them to be converted to the air-to-air tanker role. The Vulcan fleet still had many hours of fatigue life left in its airframes and the RAF decided to retain its services as a tactical or strategic bomber. The last nuclear deterrent (*Blue Steel*) sortie was performed by a 617 Squadron Vulcan on December 21, 1970. The ageing stand-off weapon had remained in service longer than expected because work to develop its planned replacement, the US-built *Skybolt* air-launched missile was cancelled in December 1962. Britain had chosen to base its entire 1960s deterrent force on *Skybolt*, and its cancellation led to a major disagreement between the UK and US, known today as the Skybolt Crisis. >>

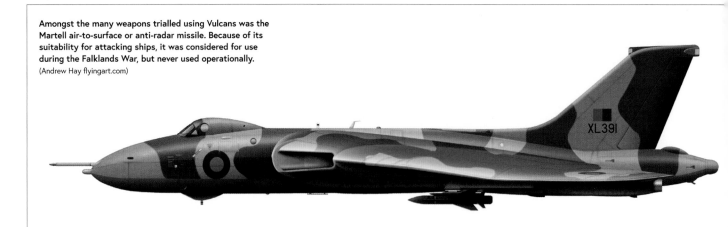

Amongst the many weapons trialled using Vulcans was the Martell air-to-surface or anti-radar missile. Because of its suitability for attacking ships, it was considered for use during the Falklands War, but never used operationally.
(Andrew Hay flyingart.com)

RIGHT: Vulcan B.2, XM574 of 617 Sqn, on detachment to Luqa, Malta, in 1977, shows the matt camouflage upper surfaces and light grey undersides introduced in 1972, along with subdued blue-and-red-only roundels.
(KEY Archive)

BELOW: Vulcan crew participated in numerous *Red Flag* exercises in the United States. Here a 44 Squadron machine departs Nellis AFB, Nevada, during the 1980 event. Note the darker wraparound' camouflage scheme.

Skybolt's cancellation had led the UK to anticipate the need for a stop-gap weapon between the retirement of *Blue Steel* and the eventual introduction of a submarine-based system. The stopgap was a tactical nuclear bomb, the WE.177, which was still in use when *Blue Steel* was finally withdrawn. It enabled the RAF to retain a tactical nuclear strike capability and the Vulcan force was one of the aircraft types chosen to carry it. The bomb was used as a laydown weapon – delivered either by ballistic /loft mode or by retarded (parachute-attached) methods.

Deliveries of the early version – the WE.177A – began in 1966 and trials were performed using a Vulcan B.2 from the Cottesmore Wing. A later version, the WE.177C, was also carried by Buccaneers and Sea Harriers until the weapon was completely withdrawn from use in 1992. The conversion to low level operations – still together with Victors at this stage – resulted in the fitting of new electronic countermeasures equipment, side scanning radar, moving map ground position indicators and terrain following radar.

After years of maximum altitude flying the Vulcan – and for a shorter time, the Victor – became far more common sights, as they thundered across the UK's more remote areas where training sorties were allowed.

A handful of Vulcans were modified to perform a maritime / strategic radar reconnaissance role which they undertook between 1973-1982.

Despite being effectively redundant, it was to be more than a decade before any prospects of a replacement that could offer all the Vulcan's capabilities – the Panavia Tornado – finally emerged although the new jet would not enter service until 1986.

The Vulcan's retirement process began in late 1981. The Vulcan units at Scampton began to slowly wind down their operations and many aircraft were either delivered to museums or other RAF airfields for use as crew / fire training aids. Back then, the RAF was offering these multi-million-pound deltas – albeit with much operational equipment removed – for just £5,500, including delivery, providing you had a suitable runway to take delivery of your own personal V-bomber!

The reconnaissance Vulcans from 27 Squadron were also retired and most of the remaining airframes were gathered at Waddington awaiting their fate. Many were scrapped or burnt on site, but just as the last Vulcans were about to fly their final sorties, Argentina's invasion of the Falkland Islands changed everything. Urgent plans were drawn-up to evaluate low-range operations over the South Atlantic and the aged Vulcan fleet was gifted a last-gasp opportunity to go enter a real shooting match.

BRITISH AVIATION
The First Half-Century - *In Colour*

JUST £25

HARDBACK, 192 PAGES

The first half of the 20th century saw the birth of the aeroplane and its development as an instrument of war and commerce. Within five decades, contraptions barely able to take to the air had given way to jet-powered aircraft, a rate of technological advance unparalleled in any other field. It was the period when Great Britain's aviation industry was established and grew to its zenith.

With over 170 period images, carefully colourised, this book chronicles the wide variety of aircraft produced in Great Britain before 1950, portraying them in their full glory once more.

A Day with the Dambusters

Shortly before the Vulcan was due to be retired from RAF service, aviation journalist **Malcolm English** was given the once-in-a-lifetime opportunity to join a practise bombing mission.

The RAF's most famous bomber squadron, 617, was formed on March 21, 1943, at RAF Scampton, Lincolnshire, under the command of Wing Commander Guy Gibson. Its first operation, the daring low-level raid upon the Ruhr dams, is now legendary and has cemented the Dambusters' place in the nation's history. Post-war, it re-rolled for jet warfare, converting to Canberras in 1952 and continued to operate them until disbandment in 1955.

On May 1, 1958, the Dambusters reformed at Scampton with Vulcan B.1s, and the following year was presented with its standard by the Queen Mother. The squadron reequipped with the Vulcan B.2s in early 1962 and became the first to be armed with the then state-of-the-art *Blue Steel* stand-off bombs. It continued in the strategic bombing role until the last *Blue Steel* sortie in December 1970.

With a maximum speed of around 625 mph and a cruising speed of 607 mph at 50,000ft the Vulcan B.1 was a challenging target for attacking fighters of 1950s vintage. However, this situation soon changed, particularly the Delta-jet's vulnerability to improved surface-to-air missiles. Hence the introduction of the Vulcan B.2 with its numerous new electronic countermeasures and stand-off bombing capability.

More effective Soviet defences also forced the Vulcans to adapt to a low-level strike role and as a further aid in this mission the aircraft supper surfaces were camouflaged; earlier schemes were overall anti-radiation white. Further changes were made in 1979 when the Vulcan fleet began to receive an overall dark green and dark grey scheme which made it even more difficult for the Vulcan to be spotted by eye, particularly during manoeuvres with large angles of bank. To fly the aircraft at such low altitudes and in conditions of poor visibility a terrain following radar (TFR) was installed. »

BELOW:
617 Squadron's XM574, moments from touchdown at RAF Honington 1978. (Malcom English)

This enabled the pilot to follow the contours of the terrain at a pre-selected height. External evidence of the TFR is a radar pod on the nose of the aircraft.

POST-WAR DETERRENT ROLES

Following the introduction of the *Polaris* ballistic missiles carried by Royal Navy submarines from 1967, the RAF relinquished its strategic nuclear deterrent role. The V-force, which then included Victors as well as Vulcans, was then re-armed with nuclear or conventional gravity bombs for use against tactical targets. The Vulcan's maximum conventional load is 21 x 1,000lb bombs.

Shortly before 617's Vulcan-era disbandment on December 31, 1991, I was given the privilege of visiting the squadron to fly on a typical training sortie.

Having passed what was then Scampton's 'gate guardian' Avro Lancaster NX611 (now the centrepiece of the Lincolnshire Aviation Heritage Museum at East Kirkby), I was taken first to the Vulcan escape rig. Of the five Vulcan crew members, only two, the pilot and co-pilot, were afforded the luxury of ejection seats. In an emergency the three rear crew members plus any additional personnel, such as instructors – and on this occasion yours truly – would have to vacate the aircraft via the entrance door / escape hatch which is under the front fuselage.

A proposal to fit ejection seats for all crew members was considered in 1964, mainly to improve the rear crew's chances of survival in low-level emergencies. However, it was rejected, largely I suspect on grounds of costs, which would have been about £35,000 per aircraft at that time. Subsequent fatalities caused the question to be raised again, but without result.

Arriving at the escape rig – a mock-up fuselage – I was introduced to Flight Lieutenant Alan Walker and Squadron Leader Mike Straw; Alan and Mike were to be my pilot and radar navigator, respectively. They began by explaining how to strap on a back-type parachute and personal survival pack (PSP). Then, shedding my parachute and PSP, I climbed into the Vulcan.

Considering the Vulcan's bulk, the crew compartment was surprisingly small. The three rear-crewmembers sit on aft-facing seats in front of one long table, above which is a myriad of knobs, switches, gauges, dials, and cathode ray tubes. Forward of the entrance/escape hatch, the pilots sit side by side under a fighter-type bubble canopy. My seat was a conveniently sculpted area of the airframe forming a step on the port side of the compartment immediately forward of the air electronics officer (AEO's) seat.

After showing me how to fasten up oxygen, an intercom lead and parachute connections, Mike went on to describe the escape procedures. If the aircraft had to be vacated after a wheels-up landing or a runway overrun, the way out would be upward. This would mean climbing up to the flight deck, squeezing between the ejection seats and then either sliding down the side of the fuselage or climbing back across it.

Baling-out would be even more exciting. On the command "abandon aircraft" Mike would lower the escape hatch and slide down it to be first out. I would follow and close behind would be the navigator plotter and AEO. Ejecting or baling-out is a serious enough business at the best of times. Knowing that two lives could depend on my rapid egress was a sobering thought and I paid the upmost attention to Mike's briefing. The escape hatch is situated directly forward of the nose undercarriage, so baling-out while the wheels are down could be a pretty rough experience. I wasn't too consoled by the assurance that tests with dummies had proved the method; under certain conditions they bounced off the wheels en route!

After picking up flying clothing from the stores I was taken to the safety equipment section for a briefing on the oxygen system, parachute, and dinghy. We then went to the flight planning room where I was introduced to the rest of the crew, Flight Lieutenant Jim Rooney, co-pilot; Flight Lieutenant Paul West, navigator plotter; and Flight Lieutenant Gordon Dearlove, AEO.

OUR MISSION

Alan Walker outlined the mission and led us through the pre-flight brief. Our sortie was to conduct simulated low-level strikes against three targets on the Western Isles of Scotland. The targets were a small bridge straddling a stream on the west side of the island of Mull, one tree on the corner of a wood on the island of Skye and an airfield building at Stornoway on the Isle of Lewis. I thought the second target was a joke, but ought to have known better. Radar and visual attacks were planned for the first two targets respectively, with an option for Stornoway.

It was interesting to note that because of the limited visibility from the Vulcan's flight deck, the aircraft was only allowed to fly low-level through a few well-defined routes; its size was a contributing factor to that restriction. The brief ended with a last word from Gordon to warn the AEO of any bird strike threats. In such an event he would start the airborne auxiliary powerplant. This would provide emergency electrical services in the case of bird ingestion causing engine failures. We then went to the mess for a light but welcome breakfast.

Walking out to our aircraft XL318, I took the opportunity to photograph the Vulcans on the dispersal. At the time of my visit three aircraft were unavailable for photography. Two were on detachment in Denmark for exercise *Brown Falcon* and one was under guard, armed with a practise special weapon.

During the external pre-flight check, I was shown the aircraft's huge bomb bay. With the exception of a 5,500lb-capacity saddle tank in the front, which took up surprisingly little room, it was empty.

In the days when 617 Squadron operated in the conventional bombing role, 12x28lb practise bombs were normally carried on training sorties. When tasked with a nuclear strike role, however, only four practise bombs were usually carried. Our bombing accuracy was to be analysed from film taken with a vertically mounted F-95 camera mounted above the bomb aimer's window.

The order of boarding was pilots first, then the rear crew and me last. While Mike Straw helped me to fasten on my parachute and PSP and connect the intercom lead and oxygen supply, the rest of the crew busied themselves with their pre-flight checks. The rear crew positions were radar navigator, starboard seat; radar plotter in the centre and AEO on the port side. To facilitate rapid egress their seats swivel and each one had an assisted cushion to help push its occupant to his feet under conditions of positive 'G'.

At 1230 hours the first of XL318's four Olympus 200 series engines was started with the remainder spooling-up in quick succession. Although each Olympus can produce 17,000lb of thrust, the engine noise was barely audible through my helmet. The crew access door was closed and at 1240 we began to taxi. After moving forward a few feet the brakes and nosewheel steering were checked and satisfactory.

The pre-take-off checks were completed before reaching the runway and as we aligned with the centreline the brakes were applied and throttles opened to 80%. At 1247, with the engines stabilised, the brakes were released, and the throttles advanced to give full thrust.

With Jim Rooney at the controls, we rotated at 150kts and climbed out into the circuit at 160kts. Our all-up weight at take-off was 180,000lb. During the turn downwind for our heavyweight circuit, Mike closed one set of curtains which sealed off the rear crew compartment from the flight deck. Looking over his shoulder at the H2S radar scope while we performed a radar approach, I was surprised at the clarity of the airfield image. So much so that I voiced the hope that a potential enemy does not have radar maps of our airfields. I gathered from the response that it was a forlorn one.

Digressing slightly but remembering 617 Squadron's Pathfinder role during World War Two, the effectiveness of toned down-airfields may be appreciably reduced if a radar pathfinder led the attacker. Admittedly we were somewhat higher than an attacking aircraft might be, and we were in a jam-free environment. However, those advantages would have been somewhat offset by the Vulcan's antiquated H2S radar. »

During our transit up the east coast, I occupied my time between peering at Mike's radarscope and between the pilots' ejection seats at the outside world some 39,000ft below. Mike and Paul gave me a demonstration of the aircraft's navigation equipment, including the radar bombing mode. By feeding target coordinates into the bombing computer, it could output left and right steer commands to the pilot.

Loaded down with parachute and PSP, after a short while simply standing up in the Vulcan became tiring; and looking out of the cockpit window was exhausting. This necessitated wedging myself in a narrow gap between the ejection seats while balancing on a ladder leading up to the flight deck. To make this position even more uncomfortable, the Avro designers placed a bulkhead behind the seats which snags a parachute pack. By standing as high as possible on the ladder, I could just see the flight-refuelling probe over the nose of the aircraft. Probes were fitted to all the Vulcan fleet but at that time inflight refuelling was not practised.

We began to let down over Loch Ness, descending on a westerly heading and taking care not to fly below safety height. While over land this was defined as 1,500 feet plus 10% above the highest terrain point within 35 miles. Continuing west, Mike gave us radar confirmation that we were over the sea. Therefore, it was safe to descend to 800 feet.

There was then a constant dialogue between pilots and navigators, the pilots warning of cloud and Mike drawing their attention to ships and rocks appearing on his radar. Gordon was receiving considerable electronic countermeasures (ECM) jamming from Stornoway some of which could be heard over the intercom. Unfortunately, I was unable to hear it as my intercom connection had broken!

The flight so far had been remarkably smooth, so when Alan called out that we were approaching Tiree, I hauled myself up to the flight deck to watch. This was against Mike's advice to stay sat down during the low-level penetration "otherwise you will be tired out". I was to regret it! On request from the air traffic control tower, we conducted a low fly-past of Tiree airfield. Although I

had only been on the ladder for some 15 minutes, I was sweating with exertion.

RUN-IN TO THE TARGET

At 1440 the navigators advised that we were 15 miles from the first target. From then on, the intercom was alive with: "accelerating now…12 miles to target… coast at five (Isle of Mull) …target at ten (bridge)…correction left…looks good…five miles…two miles…going too fast…wings level…switches made…doors open…contact (pilot has visual sight of the target) …sharp left…half second…3,2,1, now!" Then it was: "Doors closed…watch the high ground…stay in the valley." The 'bomb' was released at 320kts and 300ft and considering the Vulcan's low wing loading the running was quite smooth. However, when the bomb doors were open the ride was like driving over cobblestones.

The bomb doors had just been closed when we flew into turbulence and I, together with maps and plotting instruments became airborne. My 'bone-dome' prevented what would otherwise have been a crack on the head as it hit the structure. Then my PSP literally cushioned the blow as the aircraft came up to meet me again. Assuring the concerned crew that I was okay, we pressed on north along the low-level route past Tobermory on the island of Mull. Our speed had been reduced to 220kts and the wings levelled for one of Mike's radar fixes when he called: "ship ahead". Alan identified it as a minesweeper, coasted to it and then let the Royal Navy know we had arrived by firewalling the throttles as we passed over. If its crew read this perhaps Alan's hand slipped!

Our second target was attacked visually at the same height and speed as the first. The approach was through what the crew called 'Death Valley' on the Isle of Skye. This time the running was quite bumpy due to turbulence from the hills around us. During the ten miles to our target (the tree) Alan map read, calling out his turn points along with the way. At 3 1/2 miles the bomb doors were opened with the accompanying vibration. I then heard: "camera on…3, 2, 1, bombs gone, close doors" and we were heading out to Stornoway for target number three.

ABOVE: **The cockpit of XL318, the 'author's bomber' for the day. This aircraft is now preserved at the RAF Museum, Hendon.**
(Malcolm English)

Fatigue is closely monitored on all RAF aircraft and the Vulcan fleet carried accelerometers to measure the number of times a certain value of 'G-force' was exceeded. In that way the fatigue life of each Vulcan was recorded. During our mock attack on Skye XL318 clocked up 118 counts, as did my stomach! I was beginning to sympathise with the definition of a Vulcan flight given to me, prior to my sortie, by the crew: "It's like sitting in a spin dryer in a darkened room with someone beating the sides with a broom handle."

It was decided to perform a radar approach and manual release on Stornoway and at 1505 and 25 miles from our target Alan requested our clearance from the tower. Shortly after a call came from the left-hand seat to "floor it" and we accelerated in to the airfield. Instead of a direct attack we flew initially to an offset point some seven miles out. At six miles Mike made some necessary corrections to the ballistics computer.

Then, over the intercom came the chant: "speed's good… five miles…four miles…turn right, right…go visual". I felt the familiar cobblestones as the bomb doors opened and Alan called: "3,2,1 now!" Through the bomber aimer's window, I saw airfield buildings flash by and then it was all over, bar the shouting, which came from the rear. "Sorry Alan I pointed at the wrong b…. building." As it was only feet from the intended target, the error certainly would not have mattered had we dropped a live store. Nevertheless, there were principles and standards at stake and Mike was the butt of some leg-pulling during the flight home.

En route to our practise diversion to Lossiemouth, Norman discovered that a fuse had blown causing a fuel pump failure. It was not a serious failure and could have been remedied in flight had the crew wanted to. At 4,000ft on the approach to Lossiemouth we hit slight turbulence but had passed through it at 3,000ft. I heard the tower inform us of one aircraft ahead and then lost contact as my intercom lead separated; this had been a nuisance

throughout the flight. However, I managed to reconnect it in time to hear that there were Harriers, Buccaneers, Jaguars, and a Victor on the airfield. We conducted an overshoot at 100ft followed by an impressive acceleration and climb.

With a fuel load of 30,000lb we set course for Scampton. As the lunch boxes came out, I was more than satisfied with the light snack of chocolate, apple, and milk. Our transit height was a steady 41,000ft until, at 1620, we began to descend. To hold a descent speed of 250kts the air brakes were extended, the only indications being a mild buffet. At 1640, after a flight time of four hours, we touch down on runway 23. Aerodynamic braking was used to minimise brake wear and the nose lowered gently at around 80kts. Again, to conserve the brakes the outboard engines were shut down while we taxied to the dispersal.

The squadron has continued the tradition of excellence set by its World War Two predecessors. In the Vulcan days this was demonstrated by its performance in bombing competitions and *Red Flag* exercises. The latter confirmed the credibility of the Vulcan and its performance against multiple threats including its ability to penetrate fighter defences. Nevertheless, age, advances in technology, improved threats and changes in the operational requirements all contributed to the retirement of this great aeroplane.

Of course, 617 went on to fly the Tornado from 1982 until disbandment in 2014, reforming two years later to fly the F-35B Lightning II at RAF Marham.

As for 'my' Vulcan, XL318, it made its last flight with 617 Squadron on December 11, 1981, flying over the Derwent Reservoir which the original Dambusters had used to practise their skills prior to their 1943 dams' attacks. Earmarked for preservation, XL318 was dismantled and transported to the RAF Museum at Hendon where she is still on display today.

XM607

First in Anger

Just as the Vulcan and Victor's operational sunset approached, war clouds appeared on the horizon and the V-Force jets were thrust into a real shooting war. **Chris Pierce** recalls the daring *Black Buck* raid on Port Stanley Airfield.

When the Vulcan and Victor were thought to be in their twilight years of service, Britain's armed forces were primarily focused on defending the country and its NATO allies against the danger posed by the Soviet Union. Despite the long-running dispute about the Falklands sovereignty, their remoteness from the UK ensured they were not at the forefront of British military thinking. However, the Argentine military dictatorship of the day was secretly planning to invade the islands to boost its flagging popularity by generating a wave of jingoism. By 1982, the Malvinas – as they are known to Argentina – were set to be 'reclaimed' by its armed forces.

Studies of the Falklands Islands' remote location in the South Atlantic led British military chiefs to assume that they were indefensible in strategic terms and only a nominal British force was stationed there. In late March

1982, Argentine forces prepared for an invasion with their troops hiding their intentions while performing clandestine 'exercises'. On the late evening of April 1, Argentina launched *Operation Rosario* and members of its special forces were the first to set foot on the islands, south of Port Stanley. Dawn would bring the full invasion. A fierce but brief firefight lasted for a few hours but, hopelessly outnumbered, the token British force's only realistic option was to lay down its arms. For a brief period, some captured British Royal Marines were forced to lie face down on the floor and filmed for propaganda purposes, with the aim of showing that the British were beaten. However, when the images were broadcast in the UK, instead of convincing the British people that the battle was over, with Argentina victorious, a sense of outrage galvanised public and political opinion into demanding the islands' recapture. The British government reacted swiftly. »

MAIN PICTURE:
During the Falklands conflict, air-to-air refuelling was to prove invaluable when Avro Vulcan B.2 XM607 made the first of several raids by 101 Sqn on the vital airfield at Port Stanley on the Falkland Islands. Significantly, the Chief of the Air Staff at the time was Michael Beetham, who had done so much to prove the concept more than 20 years previously.
(KEY Archive)

LONG RANGE BOMBING

Argentinian military codes had been broken and in the month before the invasion, the British intelligence services were gradually collating information about the Latin American nation's manoeuvres in the South Atlantic. As part of its normal planning routine, the Royal Air Force studied potential long- and ultra-long air operations in support of its interests and those of its allies. Such location scenarios included the Falkland Islands, but it was deemed that the RAF could do little to support the Royal Navy and British troops in the South Atlantic in a shooting war. The nearest airbase available to British forces was Wideawake airfield on Ascension Island, near the equator, almost halfway between the UK and Falklands Islands. Ascension was a British territory, and its airfield boasted a 10,000ft runway, making it perfect to accomodate the heavily laden aircraft essential for the 3,300nm flight from the UK and the extra 3,700nm to the Falklands. The operational conditions were fraught with difficulties but the cries for military action overruled everything else. The RAF's air-to-air refuelling capability would a be a critical factor in any long-range bombing raids conducted. The RAF was able to deploy its air-to-air tanker fleet to Ascension Island at remarkably short notice (see *Warzones!*) along with its Vulcan bombers.

While US-led diplomatic efforts sought to diffuse the politically charged situation, British forces were busy consolidating their tactics and selecting potential targets.

The biggest threat to the British Task Force sailing to reclaim the Islands would be Argentinian fighter aircraft operating from Port Stanley airfield. If Stanley's runway could be disabled, or its full length effectively reduced in some way, it would prevent the fast jets of Argentina's Fuerza Aérea from using Stanley. They would be forced to fly from airbases in Argentina, significantly lowering their effective combat radius.

The key question was, could a Vulcan reach Stanley undetected? If discovered inbound to the target it would almost certainly be destroyed by the airfield's defences. Arguably, this was going to be RAF's most daring bombing operation since the famous Dambusters' raid of 1943. It would definitely be its longest.

Record-breaker

The first Vulcan bombing raid, targeting Port Stanley airfield began in the early hours of May 1 and was called *Operation Black Buck 1*. Eleven Victor tankers would take part for the outbound journey and a further five for the return. Two Vulcans were deployed, each loaded with 21x1,000lb bombs, a primary aircraft (XM598) and a

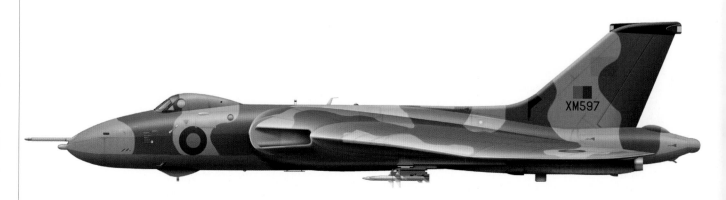

reserve (XM607) and these taxied out at Wideawake while ahead of them four Victors took off at one-minute intervals in the first wave. The Vulcans followed and behind them the second wave of seven Victors took off, both waves climbing to 27,000ft and heading south. During the climb, the primary Vulcan reported problems with cabin pressurisation and had to abort, making the reserve aircraft, XM607, captained by Flight Lieutenant Martin Withers the spearhead of the operation.

Settling at 33,000ft, the two formations continued towards the Falklands, the plan being to conduct five refuels of the Vulcan but in the end six were needed. As the waves progressed, one Victor after another peeled off and returned to Ascension until there were only two Victors and the Vulcan remaining. Victor K.2 XH669 captained by Flight Lieutenant S Biglands and XL189 being flown by Squadron Leader Bob Tuxford. The weather steadily deteriorated as they approached the Falklands, Tuxford's final refuel of Vulcan B.2, XM607 was conducted and then the plan was to refuel Biglands' aircraft and then turn for home. After the Vulcan was successfully topped up, the weather continued to get worse as Tuxford positioned himself to refuel the XH669. As Biglands approached, he was greeted with the sight of a 'dancing' refuelling basket which was being buffeted around 20ft in any one direction. Despite this, Biglands managed to get his refuelling probe in the basket only to damage the probe in the process, stopping the transfer of any fuel. A quick decision had to made, Tuxford deciding to reverse the planned roles of the two Victors and take on fuel from Biglands aircraft instead and support the Vulcan. Biglands transferred as much as could, leaving sufficient to return to Ascension as he was no longer able to be refuelled. Tuxford refuelling the Vulcan again, his decision enabling *Black Buck 1* to continue to its target, but not leaving sufficient fuel for a safe return to Wideawake. In the meantime, Victors from the first wave were landing back at Wideawake and one tanker was quickly turned

BELOW: **The delivery aircraft for** *Black Buck 1*, **XM607 was retired to Waddington at the end of its RAF Career.** (J Springfield)

Lessons learned

Many lessons were learned by the tanker force before *Black Buck 2* was launched late on May 3. A slightly different approach was conducted for this operation, two smaller waves supported a single Vulcan, XM507 again, this time captained by Squadron Leader R Reeve. The first wave consisted of the Vulcan and its primary refuellers which accompanied the bomber two-thirds of way to the target before all turned home. In the meantime, a second wave, which only took off five minutes later from Wideawake flew at a higher altitude and higher speed, catching up with the Vulcan much further along the route. The final objective was to leave a single full tanker with the Vulcan so that the bomber could be fully refuelled before attacking the target, which was again, Port Stanley airfield. The plan worked as intended and once again the airfield was successfully bombed, this time damage being caused to infrastructure and various Argentine equipment. The technique was retained for the five *Black Buck* raids that followed, although one was cancelled due to a technical failure.

around so that it could meet Tuxford's aircraft. With only 30 minutes of fuel remaining, and still 600 miles away from Ascension, Tuxford was met by the hugely welcome sight of another Victor in position to transfer fuel so they too could get back safely to Wideawake.

In the meantime, Vulcan XM507 continued to its target, descending to 300ft to avoid radar on approach and then climbed to 8,000ft. At 0438, all 21 bombs were delivered in the space of five seconds, one of them crucially exploding in the middle of the main runway. The British had announced their presence and intent with a single raid.

It was now time to set course back to Wideawake and once again the well-orchestrated tanker plan worked, the first refuel taking place off the Brazilian coast. By the time XM607 landed at Wideawake at 1452, it had taken on fuel 17 times and was airborne for 15 hours 45 minutes and had flown a distance of 9,200 miles. It was the longest non-stop bombing raid in history and the record stood until surpassed by a United States Air Force B.2 stealth bomber during the Afghanistan campaign more than two decades later.

Regardless of the sterling work that the Vulcan conducted during the Falklands campaign, the planned rundown of the type from RAF service remained on track. Now all congregated at RAF Waddington, Lincolnshire, 101 Squadron and later 44 Squadron's disbandment would play out during August and December 1982. However, the fate of 50 Squadron, took an unusual turn thanks to a serious lack of tanker aircraft. A combination of the long-range Vulcan operations against the Falklands and the needs of Nimrod and Hercules aircraft had put a great strain on the Victor tanker fleet, reducing the fatigue life of the type by some margin. Plans were already in place prior to the Falklands to increase the tanker capability of the RAF with the purchase of all the recently retired British Airways Vickers VC10s, a type the service was no stranger to and an ideal aircraft for conversion. Unfortunately, the conversion of a purely civilian airliner to a military in-flight refuelling tanker was not a straightforward exercise, modifications

being extensive, not to mention that the development programme had been delayed following an incident which damaged the first aircraft, thanks to a flaying hose and drogue. Immediately after the Falklands conflict a further nine Tristar airliners had also been purchased, three of them ex-Pan Am for passenger duties and six from British Airways. The latter half dozen was penned in at Marshalls of Cambridge for conversion to tanker aircraft. Overall, the near future of the RAF's tanker force was looking good, but the service needed tankers immediately and it would be the Vulcan that provided a much-needed stopgap.

MODIFICATION 2600

The task to convert the Vulcan into a tanker was given to British Aerospace (BAe) at Woodford, the work being officially called Modification 2600. The first task was to survey a Vulcan to ascertain how a Hose Drum Unit (HDU) could be installed into the airframe, with least disruption. Conveniently, BAe had its own Vulcan which had only arrived, ex-Waddington Wing, on March 12, 1982. XM603, a Vulcan B.2 was put through a comprehensive survey, all eyes being drawn to the large ECM housing at the tip of the rear fuselage, which was deemed to be large enough to house an HDU, albeit a sizeable proportion of the unit would be protruding from the lower rear fuselage; it would not be pretty!

The bones of Modification 2600 deemed that six Vulcans would be converted, the bulk of the work including the reinstatement of the bomb-bay centre position fuel tank connectors and the installation of the HDU (Flight Refuelling Mk.17B), destined for the VC10 programme. All remnants of the ECM systems and the vapour-cycle cooling pack (VCCP) and its matrix cooler (located on the outside of the aircraft) were removed. There was just sufficient stock of 'A' and 'E' type bomb-bay fuel tanks, all cylindrical type for the six aircraft chosen. Within the old ECM bay, new mountings and structural support beams were installed to carry the HDU. To smooth the airflow over the protruding section of the HDU, what only can be described as an 'inelegant piece of kit,' was immediately described by those around as the 'Council Skip' (later also tagged the 'dog house'). The 'skip,' designed by chief designer military, Alan Clegg, was made of angle iron and sheet aluminium and as mentioned earlier it was not pretty but did the job perfectly. Beneath the skip was a tail bumper arm, within it was a microswitch linked to the cockpit which illuminated when the aircraft's angle of attack was too high; an easy scenario to be in when taking off and landing the Vulcan. There was a moveable flap at the front of the 'skip' to gain access to various parts of the system and either side of the drogue aperture was a set of small 'traffic lights' in red, amber and green. The three bomb-bay tanks were all connected to the HDU via new pipework, although these gained access to the rear fuselage by making use of the long redundant aperture in the rear bulkhead once used for the *Blue Steel* missile. »

BELOW: **Easy does it! There is a great deal of professional pride in being able to 'prod the basket' at the first attempt.** (Malcolm English)

The Stopgap Tanker

In the twilight of her service years the Vulcan received her final tasking, explains **Chris Pierce**.

The size of the aperture which the drogue tucked into was critical, but its final shape was achieved by slowly carving large blocks of Styrofoam with Alan Clegg's penknife before the perfect shape was reached.

Further modifications included non-return valves in the bomb-bay tanks to ensure that no fuel meant for the recipient was used by the Vulcan tanker. Capable of carrying up to 24,000lb of fuel, the Vulcan could not burn this off in the event of an emergency. However, using the tanks own pumps, this fuel could be vented off at a rate of 360 gallons per minute. The new fuel system was controlled electrically and as a result additional new looms had to be installed as well as a much improved fire detection and suppression system for the old bomb bay area. Control of the fuel tank pumps was installed in the retractable (Panel 5P) fuel control console located between the pilot and co-pilot, each tank having its own switches.

The Navigator Radar operator's panel was also modified, it now included switches and indicators for the HDU bay heating and temperature controls and a 'press-to-test' for the bomb-bay temperature. The Navigator Plotter's position was also changed to include an HDU monitoring panel. An additional panel kept an eye on the HDU bleed air and incorporated a 'press-to-transmit' for the benefit of aircraft requiring fuel. Except for the HDU primary control panel, which was produced by Flight Refuelling Ltd., BAe produced all panels. The HDU primary control panel presented the all-important fuel flow rate, quantity issued, power controls, extent of hose deployed and an emergency device that could chop the hose if things went awry.

All tanker aircraft required markings under their rear fuselage to help guide the receiving pilot to connect to the trailing hose and drogue. No two tankers were the same from underneath at altitude and a unique design for the Vulcan was produced. Chief test pilot 'Robby' Robinson was instrumental in the design and the following is an excerpt from his excellent book *Avro One*: "The markings under the Vulcan and the night lighting threw up some interesting aspects. I was asked to suggest what was necessary to provide markings to guide the receiver

BELOW: **An English Electric Lightning, renowned for being a permanently fuel-thirsty machine, receives a top-up while two Jaguar pilots look on.** (Malcolm English)

pilots. All tankers have such markings that indicate to a pilot when he is lined up with the drogue and to show the correct angle of approach. I quickly sketched how this could be done; a straight red line outlined in white ran up the centre of the skip and continued along the rear of the aircraft's fuselage, and this provided line up. Another similar line was drawn across the skip and when the receiver was approaching at the correct angle this line joined up with two similar lines, one on each wing trailing edge. This all proved to be excellent in practice, but the design process had its ridiculous side. Passers-by were highly amused by the sight of a group of middle-aged men in their business suits lying on the ground under the aircraft arguing about the correct placement of the lines. Night lighting involved a similar scenario. Floodlights were set into either side of the skip, and these illuminated a white painted area under the trailing edge of each wing. It was necessary to see how effective this was on the ground before we involved a receiver aircraft in an airborne trial. One must remember that all this was being done in high summer and it was only truly dark after midnight. Also, the lighting on the surrounding roads lit up the sky and made true blackness impossible. A telephone call was made to the local council and wartime necessity was quoted to ask them to turn off the streetlights in the district. They co-operated readily and so the same group of middle-aged men was seen to be lying under the aircraft again as the floodlights and traffic lights were tried out and adjusted. The verdict of the RAF pilots who eventually flew behind the Vulcan tanker was that the markings and the lighting were the best of all the tankers."

BOMBER TO TANKER IN SHORT ORDER

The details of Modification 2600 were first discussed by BAe on April 30, 1982, making the delivery of XM603 the previous month a timely and much appreciated arrival. Work was swift, the details of how the task would be conducted had been covered and confirmed by May 2 and in a mere 48 hours the first aircraft for conversion, Vulcan B.2, XH561 arrived at Woodford. BAe were lucky to have two ex-Avro Vulcan captains on the staff, Al McDicken,

"The verdict of the RAF pilots who eventually flew behind the Vulcan tanker was that the markings and the lighting were the best of all the tankers."
- Chief Test Pilot 'Robby' Robinson

ABOVE: No.50 Squadron and its Victor K.2 tankers disbanded on March 31, 1984. After that date only XH558 continued to fly with the RAF, albeit as a display aircraft.
(Malcolm English)

and Harry Nelson plus 'Robby' Robinson, who managed to bag some simulator training at Waddington so he could also take part in the flying trials.

On June 18, 1982 XH561 was ready for its first flight as a tanker and to denote this, the aircraft was redesignated as the Vulcan K.2. With Al McDicken in the left-hand seat and 'Robby' Robinson in the right, XH561 conducted its maiden flight as a tanker having only arrived at Woodford just over six weeks earlier. During the flight, the aircraft suffered a power control failure, but Robby admitted the issue was down to his error and in the hands of Al McDicken it was skilfully brought home to Woodford. The Vulcan only suffered a minor scrape of the HDU unit on landing, which was quickly repaired and flown again without trouble that afternoon.

The very first Vulcan air-to-air refuelling trial was conducted on June 22, the recipient being Nimrod MR.2, XV229 with the boss of 'B' Squadron, A&AEE, Boscombe Down, Wing Commander Ian Strachan at the controls and an equally successful refuelling sortie that same night was conducted to prove all was well. Numerous flight trials were hurriedly conducted, and the Vulcan K.2 was cleared for operational service, XH561 being delivered back to 50 Squadron at Waddington on June 23.

The second aircraft to be converted was XJ825 which arrived at Woodford on May 11, returning to Waddington as a K.2 on July 1 and XH560 followed, arriving June 15, and returning on August 28. XM571 was delivered to Woodford on May 11, returning to the sky as a K.2 on July 13 but instead of being returned to Waddington the aircraft was sent to A&AEE, Boscombe Down for clearance flying and to serve as a type example for modified Pilot's Notes. XL445 arrived at Woodford on May 25 and was converted and returned to Waddington by July 22. The final Vulcan to go through tanker conversion was XH558 which arrived at Woodford on June 30, the aircraft taking flight as a K.2 for the first time on September 3. XH558

was retained by British Aerospace for flight trials and did not return to 50 Squadron at Waddington until October 12, only 13 days later, to be sent south to Boscombe Down for additional flight trials before finally settling at Waddington again on November 30.

BRIEF SERVICE

50 Squadron's half dozen-strong Vulcan K.2 force was employed solely in the northern hemisphere. It may have appeared to be a small contribution on paper, but it was just enough to lower the pressure on the over-stretched tasking of the Victor tankers of 55 and 57 Squadrons whose commitment to the South Atlantic would continue for some time. 50 Squadron spent most of its time in support of the United Kingdom Air Defence organisation, the bulk of its work was refuelling aircraft such as the Phantom, Jaguar, Buccaneer and briefly, the Tornado. The Tanker Force Cell within the Waddington Operations Centre issued all the unit's tasking.

Its small tanker force did not remain intact for long and as planned the K.2 force was eventually replaced by the VC10. The first of the converted airliners was nearing completion in the spring of 1983 and to become operational would need an HDU from the Vulcan fleet. The first Vulcan to be stripped of its HDU was XJ825 on May 4 and over the following months, all the converted Vulcans followed suit. Each aircraft was then allocated to the Waddington Station Flight which systematically disposed of each aircraft beginning in January 1984 when XH560 was flown to Marham for spares recovery. In the meantime, the RAF's final operational Vulcan unit was disbanded at Waddington on March 31 and except for XH558, 50 Squadron's remaining aircraft were scattered for various ground support duties such as Battle Damage Repair Training and crash rescue training. XM571 was another exception as it enjoyed a period of display in Gibraltar until it was scrapped in 1990.

Vulcan Walkaround

The Vulcan B.2 on display inside the Cold War exhibition at the RAF Museum Cosford is XM598. It was selected as reserve aircraft for the bombing raids on Port Stanley airfield during the Falklands campaign and on six occasions was airborne heading for the Falklands. It was never needed since the primary aircraft was able to carry out the raid alone. It was chosen because it had originally been built to carry the *Skybolt* stand-off bomb and it proved quite easy to adapt to carry anti-radar missiles and an Electronic Counter Measures pod. The mountings for these are still fitted under the wings.

Data:	Vulcan B.2
Length:	99ft 11in (30.45m)
Wingspan:	111ft 0 in (33.83m)
Height:	27ft 1in (8.25m)
Wing Area:	3.964sq ft (368.27 m²)
Cruising speed:	Mach 0.86
Maximum speed:	Mach 0.92
Range:	4,000nm (7,408km)
Service ceiling:	60,000ft (18,288m)
Engines:	4 x Bristol Siddeley Olympus 201/301
Fuel capacity:	9,250 imp gal (42,051 lit)

MAIN PICTURE: XM598 was flown to RAF Cosford for preservation in January 1983 and moved to its current home inside the Museum's Cold War Exhibition in May 2006.
(RAF Museum Cosford)

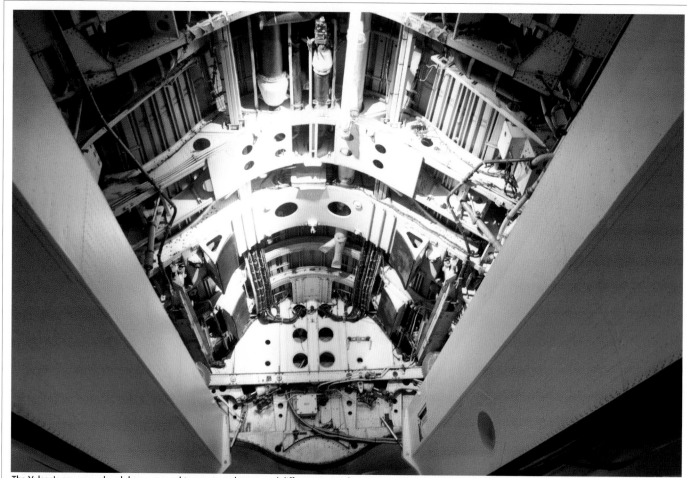

The Vulcan's cavernous bomb bay was used to accommodate several different types of munitions and other equipment during its service career. This view looks towards the rear of the aircraft and the bay has much of its 'plumbing' removed. As well as the recessed *Blue Steel* stand-off nuclear missile which sat part-in, part-out of the bay it could also hold a fuel tank at the extreme front of the bay or 21 x 1,000lb 'dumb' bombs. (Tom Allett)

The air-to-air refuelling probe. Despite the 4,000nm range achievable from internal fuel, its Falklands War tasks would not have been possible without the ability to refuel in mid-air. The blister below it is for the terrain-following radar. (Tom Allett)

The Vulcan bomb aimer's blister was really a throwback to previous generations of aircraft and its windows were rarely needed operationally. (Tom Allett)

The Vulcan B.2's extended tail section holds the electronic countermeasures (ECM) radar, and the bulge above marks the entry / exit point for the tail parachute. (Tom Allett)

Located on the starboard side of the fuselage's tail section is the air vent that is part of the avionics cooling system. (Tom Allett)

The air intake for the port wing's two Olympus engines. Note the boundary layer splitter plate at the extreme left of the intake. (Tom Allett)

The spring-loaded tail strike indicator informed the pilots when over-rotation had caused a runway tail strike. (Tom Allett)

While the design of the original V-bomber – the Valiant – had just two mainwheels under each wing, the Vulcan's heavier weight determined a total of 16 mainwheels underneath the giant delta wings. (Tom Allett)

During the Falklands War XM598 was the primary aircraft for AGM-45 Shrike missile armed anti-radar missions. The missiles were carried upon underwing pylons which are still on the underside of both wings. The mountings for these were built by 5 Squadron at RAF St Athan. (Tom Allett)

The Olympus engines' jet pipes. Later in its working life, the Olympus engine was redeveloped to power that other famous (part) British delta, Concorde. (Tom Allett)

IN PROFILE

The Vulcan

VULCAN B.2 XM597 entered RAF service in 1963 and went on participate in the Falklands War.

As one of the *Black Buck* 5 aircraft, on May 31, 1982 it fired two Shrike missiles at an Argentinian radar unit and succeeded in damaging it.

All *Black Buck* Vulcans had external weapons hardpoints under each wing. They in turn were attached to the *Skybolt* missile mountings that were built-in to each aircraft when they were manufactured but these were never used for their original purpose because the *Skybolt* programme was dropped.

Now on display at the National Museum of Flight, East Fortune, Scotland, it is one of only two Vulcans that has dropped live weapons in combat.

All profile drawings by
Andrew Hay / flyingart.co.uk

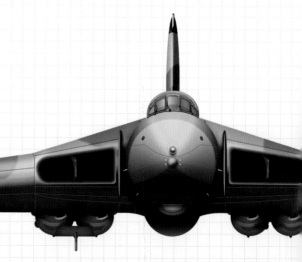

XM597

The Vulcan in Miniature

Andy Davies' Airfix Avro Vulcan B.2 depicts XM597 in the years before she became 'famous' as one of the Falklands War's *Black Buck* aircraft that took part in a series of raids against Port Stanley's airfield. The real '597 had the misfortune of its air-to-air refuelling probe being snapped off on such a mission and, with insufficient fuel to reach its Ascension base, its crew were forced to divert to Rio-Galeao Airport in Brazil causing a significant diplomatic incident.

Airfix's current 1:72 Vulcan kit provides markings for a RAF Coningsby-based B.2, XM602, of 12 Squadron in an all-white anti-nuclear flash scheme, or XM594, a *Blue Steel*-equipped 27 Squadron B.2 based at RAF Scampton, Lincolnshire.

(AWM – Andy Davies)

V-Bomber Units

ABOVE: **This superb view of the late-afternoon sun catching the 'dog-leg' of the Vulcan wing's leading edge perfectly highlights the complex shape of the ultimate design.** (Mick Dodsworth)

RAF OPERATIONAL SQUADRONS

7 Squadron
Per diem, per noctem ('By day and by night')
Aircraft
Valiant B(PR).   1 November 1956 to September 1962
Valiant B.1   January 1957 to September 1962
Valiant B(K).1   January 1957 to September 1962
Valiant B(PR)K.1   August 1961 to May 1962
Bases
Reformed at Honington (November 1, 1956); Wittering (July 26, 1960); Disbanded September 30, 1962

9 Squadron
Per noctem volamus ('We fly through the night')
Aircraft
Vulcan B.2   March 1962 to May 1982
Bases
Reformed at Coningsby (March 1, 1962); Cottesmore (November 10, 1964); Akrotiri (February 26, 1969); Waddington (January 15, 1975); Disbanded May 1, 1982

10 Sqn
Rem acu tangere ('To hit the mark')
Aircraft
Victor B.1   April 1958 to March 1964
Victor B.1A
Bases
Reformed at Cottesmore (April 15, 1958); Disbanded March 1, 1964

12 Sqn
Leads the Field
Aircraft
Vulcan B.2   July 1962 to December 1967
Bases
Reformed at Coningsby (July 1, 1962); Cottesmore (November 17, 1964); Disbanded December 31, 1967

15 Sqn
Aim Sure
Aircraft
Victor B.1   September 1958 to October 1964
Victor B.1A
Victor B.2
Bases
Reformed at Cottesmore (September 1, 1958); Disbanded October 1, 1964

18 Sqn
Animo et fide ('With courage and faith')
Aircraft
Valiant B.1   December 1958 to March 1963
Bases
Reformed at Finningley from 'C' Flight 199 Sqn (December 17, 1958); Disbanded March 31, 1963

27 Sqn
Quam celerrime ad astra ('With all speed to the Stars')
Aircraft
Vulcan B.2   April 1961 to March 1972

Bases
Reformed at Scampton (April 1, 1961); Disbanded March 29, 1972

35 Sqn
Uno animo agimus ('We act with one accord')
Aircraft
Vulcan B.2   December 1962 to Mar 1982
Bases
Reformed at Coningsby (December 1, 1962); Cottesmore (November 2, 1964); Akrotiri (January 1, 1969); Scampton (January 16, 1975); Disbanded March 1, 1982

44 Sqn
Fulmina regis iusta ('The King's thunderbolts are righteous')
Aircraft
Vulcan B.1   August 1960 to September 1967
Vulcan B.2   September 1966 to December 1982
Bases
Reformed at Waddington from 83 Sqn (August 10, 1960); Disbanded December 21, 1982

49 Sqn
Cave canem ('Beware of the Dog')
Aircraft
Valiant B.1   May 1956 to Mar 1963
Valiant B(PR).1   June 1956 to December 1964
Valiant B(K).1   November 1956 to December 1964
Bases
Reformed at Wittering (May 1, 1956); dets Christmas Island & Edinburgh Field; Marham (June 26, 1961); Disbanded May 1, 1965

50 Sqn
Sic fidem servamus ('Thus we keep faith'); Squadron badge 'From Defence to Attack'
Aircraft
Vulcan B.1   August 1961 to October 1966
Vulcan B.2   January 1966 to March 1984
Vulcan B.2(K)   June 1982 to March 1984
Bases
Reformed at Waddington from 617 Sqn (August 1, 1961); Disbanded March 31, 1984

55 Sqn
Nil nos tremefacit ('Nothing shakes us')
Aircraft
Victor B.1   September 1960 to May 1965
Victor B.1A
Victor B(K).1A   May 1965 to April 1967
Victor K.1/1A   February 1967 to August 1976
Victor K.2   July 1975 to October 1993
Bases
Reformed at Honington (September 1, 1960); Marham (May 24, 1965); Disbanded October 15, 1993

57 Sqn
Corpus non animum muto ('I change my body not my spirit')

Aircraft
Victor B.1   January 1959 to June 1966
Victor B.1A
Victor B(K).1A to K.1   February 1966 to May 1977
Victor K.2   June 1976 to June 1986
Bases
Reformed at Honington (January 1, 1959); Marham (December 1, 1965); Disbanded June 30, 1986

83 Sqn
Strike and Defend
Aircraft
Vulcan B.1   July 1957 to August 1960
Vulcan B.2   December 1960 to August 1969
Bases
Reformed at Waddington (May 21, 1957); Reduced to Cadre (August 10, 1960); Re-established at Scampton (October 1960); Disbanded August 31, 1960

90 Sqn
Celer ('Swift')
Aircraft
Valiant B(K).1   March 1957 to December 1964
Valiant B(PR).1   May 1957 to December 1960
Valiant B(PR)K.1   May 1957 to March 1961
Victor B.1A
Bases
Reformed at Honington (January 1, 57); Disbanded March 1 1965

100 Sqn
Sarang tebuan jangan dijolok ('Never stir up a hornet's nest')
Aircraft
Victor B.2   May 1962 to Sep 1968
Bases
Reformed at Wittering (May 1, 1962); Disbanded September 30, 1968

101 Sqn
Mens agitat molem ('Mind over matter')
Aircraft
Victor B.1
Vulcan B.1   October 1957 to December 1967
Vulcan B.2   December 1967 to August 1982
Bases
Reformed at Finningley (October 15, 1957); Waddington (June 26, 1961); Disbanded August 4, 1982

138 Sqn
For Freedom
Aircraft
Valiant B.1   February 1955 to March 1962
Valiant B(PR).1   March 1956 to May 1961
Valiant B(PR)K.1   March 1956 to August 1961
Valiant B(K).1   June 1956 to April 1962
Bases
Reformed at Gaydon (January 1, 1955); Wittering (July 6, 1955); Disbanded April 1, 1962

BELOW: Vickers Valiant B.1, WZ404, of 207 Squadron. The earliest Valiants flew in an all-silver colour scheme but soon adopted the all-white antiflash markings for their nuclear role. When the type was re-roled for low-level bombing tasks, the aircraft were camouflaged to make them more difficult to see over land at low-level. (Andrew Hay - flyingart.co.uk)

139 Sqn
Si placet necamus (We destroy at will)
Aircraft
Victor B.2   February 1962 to December 1968
Bases
Reformed at Wittering (February 1, 1962); Disbanded December 31, 1968

148 Sqn
Trusty
Aircraft
Valiant B(K).1   July 1956 to December 1964
Valiant B.1   December 1956 to December 1964
Valiant B(PR).1   December 1957 to December 1964
Valiant B(PR)K.1   February 1958 to December 1964
Bases
Reformed at Marham (July 1, 1956); Disbanded May 1, 1965

199 Sqn
Let tyrants tremble
Aircraft
Valiant B.1   April 1957 to December 1958
Bases
Reformed at Scampton 1957; Disbanded December 15, 1958

207 Sqn
Semper paratus ('Always prepared')
Aircraft
Valiant B(K).1   June 1956 to December 1964
Valiant B(PR).1   June 1956 to December 1964
Valiant B(PR)K.1
Valiant B.1   March 1962 to December 1964

Bases
Reformed at Marham (April 1, 1956); Disbanded May 1, 1965

214 Sqn
Ultor in umbris ('Avenging in the shadows')
Aircraft
Valiant B(PR).1   January 1956 to December 1957
Valiant B.1   March 1956 to November 1957
Valiant B(PR)K.1   April 1956 to December 1964
Valiant B(K).1   January 1957 to December 1964
Victor B(K).1A
Bases
Reformed at Marham (January 21, 1956); Disbanded March 1, 1965

543 Sqn
Valiant and Vigilant
Aircraft
Valiant B(PR).1   June 1955 to December 1964
Valiant B(PR)K.1   February 1956 to December 1963
Valiant B(K).1
Victor B.2(SR)   May 1965 to May 1974
Bases
Reformed at Gaydon (April 1, 1955); Wyton (November 18, 1955); Disbanded May 24, 1974

617 Sqn
Après moi le deluge ('After me, the flood')
Aircraft
Vulcan B.1   May 1958 to July 1961
Vulcan B.2   September 1961 to December 31, 1981
Bases
Reformed at Scampton (May 1, 1958); Disbanded December 31, 1981

BELOW:
Vickers Valiant B(PR)K.1 WZ393, of 90 Squadron, RAF. This aircraft flew operationally during the 1956 Suez crisis.
(KEY Archive)

SECOND-LINE/SUPPORT UNITS

230 OCU
Aircraft
Vulcan B.1, B.1A & B.2
Bases
Reformed at Waddington (May 31, 1956) in 1 Group
to convert crews for the Vulcan squadrons about to be
formed in Bomber Command; Finningley (June 18, 1961);
Scampton (December 8, 1969); Disbanded August 31,
1981

232 OCU
Aircraft
Valiant B.1, B(PR).1 & B(K).1, Victor B.1, B.1A, B(PR).1,
B(K).1A, B.2, K.2 & SR.2
Bases
Formed at Gaydon (February 21, 1955) in 3 Group to
provide operational training for Valiant crews; 'C' Flight
formed at Cottesmore (November 1, 1961) for Victor crews;
'C' Flight renamed Victor Training Flight (April 1, 1962);
Disbanded June 30, 1965. Reformed February 6, 1970 in
1 Group at Marham from the Victor OCU at Marham and
the Victor Training Flight at Wittering; Disbanded June 30,
1986 with the withdrawal of Victors from service

A&AEE
Aircraft
Valiant B.1, PR.1 & B(K).1, Victor B.1, B.1A, B(K).1A,
B.2 & K.2

Avro
Aircraft
Valiant B.1, Victor B.2 & Vulcan (Prototype)

Bomber Command Armament School
Formed at Wittering (August 1, 1953) to stock *Blue
Danube* atomic bombs which first arrived on November 7,
1953; Became Strike Command Armament School (April
30, 1968)

BCDU (Bomber Command Development Unit)
Aircraft
Valiant B.1 & B(K).1, Vulcan B.1A & B.2

Bases
Formed in 3 Group at Wittering (August 24, 1954);
Finningley (March 1, 1960); Redesignated Strike
Command Development Unit (April 30, 1968)

BSE
Aircraft
Valiant B.1

Decca
Aircraft
Valiant B.1

Fairey
Aircraft
Valiant B.1

Finningley Station Flight
Aircraft
Valiant B(K).1

Handley Page
Aircraft
Victor (Prototype), B.1, B.1A,
B(K).1A & B.2

Handling Squadron (A&AEE)
Aircraft
Victor B.1

Hawker Siddeley Aviation
Aircraft
Victor B.1, B.2, SR.2 & K.2

IFTU (Intensive Flying Training Unit)
Aircraft
Victor B.2

Marham Wing
Aircraft
Valiant B.1, B(PR).1, B(PR)K.1, B(K).1

Marshalls of Cambridge
Aircraft
Valiant B(K).1

Martin-Baker
Aircraft
Valiant B.1

MoA (Ministry of Aviation)
Aircraft
Victor B.2

RAE (Royal Aircraft Establishment)
Aircraft
Valiant B.1 & B(PR).1, Victor (Prototype),
B.1 & B(K).1A

Rolls-Royce
Aircraft
Valiant B.1 & Victor B.2

RRE (Radar Research Establishment)
Aircraft
Valiant B.1

RRF (Radar Reconnaissance Flight)
Aircraft
Victor B.1 & B(PR).1

ABOVE: Everybody's
favourite Vulcan?
XH558 first flew
in 1960 and was
one of the few
examples converted
for a maritime
reconnaissance
role in 1973. It was
converted again
for the airborne
tanker role in 1982
but after the type's
withdrawal from
service in 1984 it
continued with
the RAF's Vulcan
Display Flight until
1992. However, it
is best known for
its air displays
when operated by
Vulcan to the Sky
from 2007 to 2015.
(Andrew Hay -
flyingart.co.uk)

ABOVE: Handley Page Victors of 10 Squadron follow each other around the winding taxiway at RAF Cottesmore to their dispersal points in September 1958. In the foreground is XA928. (KEY Archive)

BELOW: Handley Page Victor B.2 SR XH674 of 543 Squadron. The unit flew the Victor from RAF Marham from May 1965 to May 1974. (Andrew Hay - flyingart.co.uk)

SAC Bbg Sqn (Strategic Air Command Bombing Squadron)
Aircraft
Valiant B(K).1

TTF (Tanker Training Flight)
Aircraft
Victor B.1, B.1A, B(K).1A & K.1A

Vickers-Armstrong
Aircraft
Valiant B.1, B(PR).1, B(PR)K.1, B(K).1 & B.2

Victor B.1 Ground School (Finningley)

Victor (B.2) Training Flight
Aircraft
Victor B.2   April 1962 to February 1970
Bases
Formed from 'C' Sqn 232 OCU at Cottesmore (April 1, 1962); Wittering (March 31, 1963); Disbanded February 6, 1970 into 232 OCU

Victor Flight, Wyton (or VTF (Victor Training Flight, Wyton – same unit?)
Aircraft
Victor B.2 & SR.2

Waddington Station Flight
Aircraft
Valiant B.1

Wittering Station Flight
Aircraft
Valiant B.1

Wittering Wing
Aircraft
Victor B.2

WRE (Weapons Research Establishment)
Aircraft
Valiant B.1

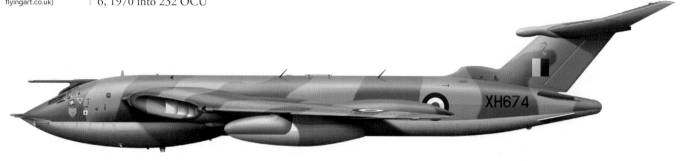